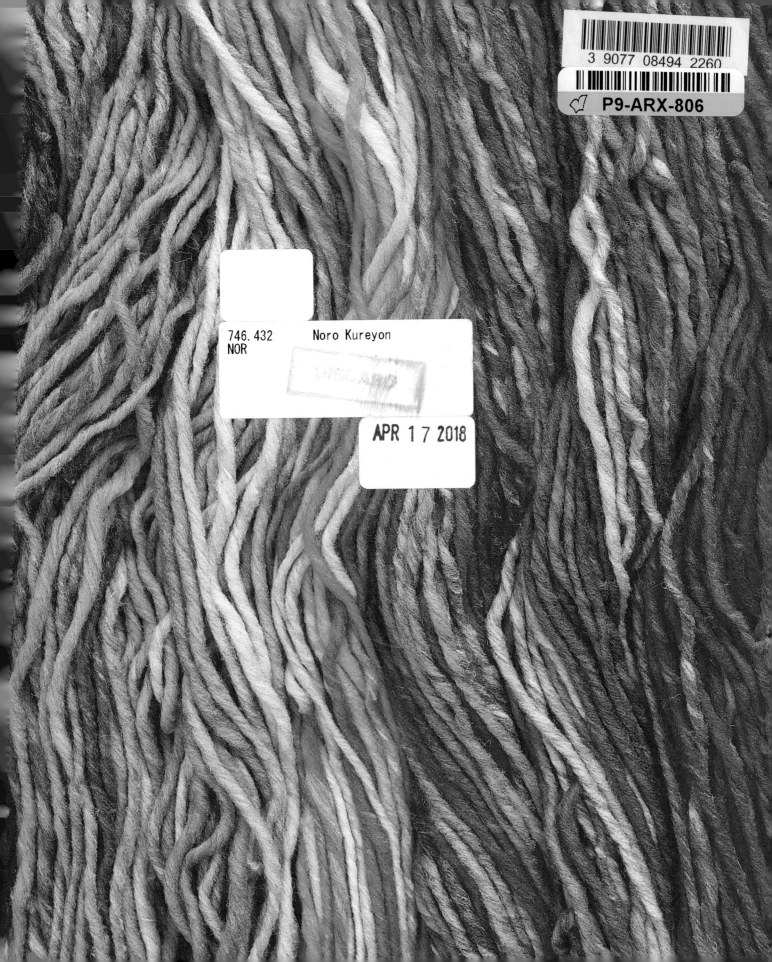

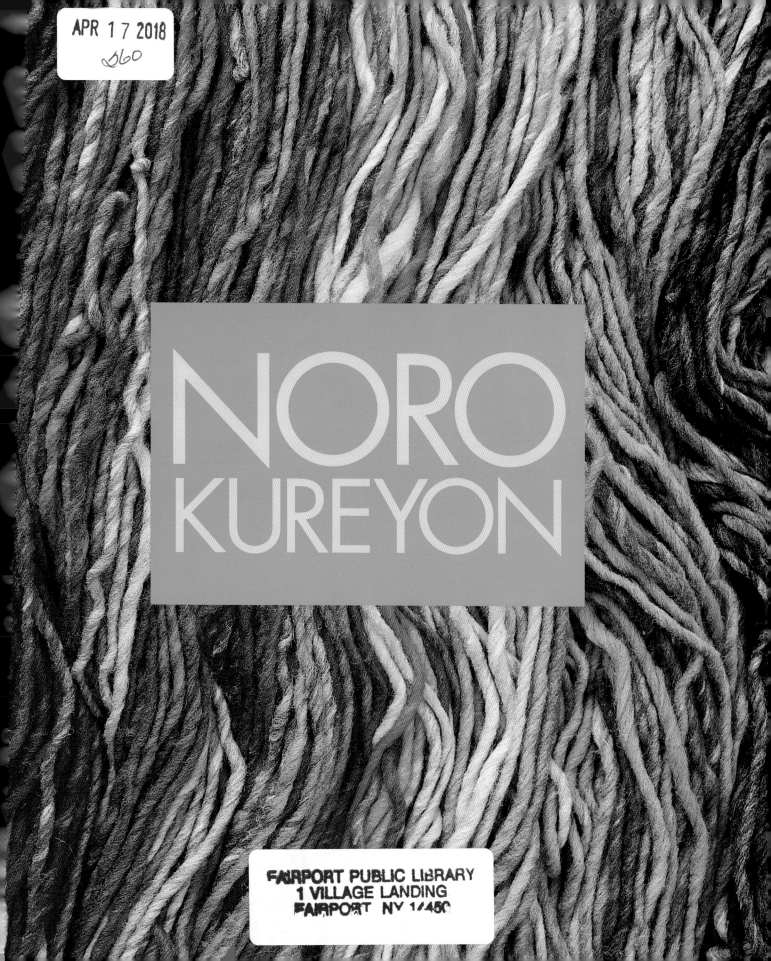

NORO
KUREYON

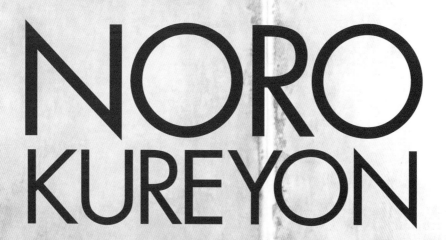

NORO
KUREYON

THE 30TH ANNIVERSARY
COLLECTION

Editor
JACOB SEIFERT

Art Director
JOE VIOR

Yarn Editor
JACLENE SINI

Supervising Patterns
Editor
CARLA SCOTT

Patterns Editors
LISA BUCCELLATO
THERESE CHYNOWETH
ROSEMARY DRYSDALE
RENEE LORION
MARI LYNN PATRICK

Technical Illustrator
LORETTA DACHMAN

Photography
JACK DEUTSCH

Stylist
JOSEFINA GARCIA

Hair and Makeup
ELENA LYAKIR

Vice President/Editorial
Director
TRISHA MALCOLM

Vice President/Publisher
CAROLINE KILMER

Production Manager
DAVID JOINNIDES

President
ART JOINNIDES

Chairman
JAY STEIN

Library of Congress Cataloging-in-Publication Data

Names: Sixth & Spring Books, editor.
Title: Noro Kureyon : the 30th anniversary collection / by the editors of Sixth&Spring Books.
Description: First edition. | New York : Sixth&Spring Books, 2018. | Includes index.
Identifiers: LCCN 2017029200 | ISBN 9781942021889 (hardcover)
Subjects: LCSH: Knitting—Patterns. | Yarn. | Eisaku Noro, Ltd.
Classification: LCC TT825 .N655 2018 | DDC 746.43/2—dc23
LC record available at https://lccn.loc.gov/2017029200

Manufactured in China

1 3 5 7 9 10 8 6 4 2

First Edition

sixth&springbooks

104 W 27th St, 3rd Floor, New York, NY 10001
www.sixthandspring.com

CONTENTS

Color Worth Remembering

Kureyon is the Japanese word for "crayon," and it only takes one look to understand why this yarn would have been given that name more than 30 years ago. Every colorway in the Kureyon family is a vibrant mix of colors that creates self-striping effects, recalling the whimsical and unbridled creativity of youth.

As each stitch is made, the knitter witnesses subtle, yet constant, changes. At first the yarn is a single color, the next moment speckles of a new hue appear, and then suddenly the yarn is a beautiful swirl of multiple colors. Just as a new color claims dominance, an additional shift begins, and the knitter cannot help but continue in joyous anticipation. Knitting with Kureyon is more than simply knitting. It is a celebration of color that can never be forgotten.

For 30 years, Noro's Kureyon has infused countless knitted pieces with unrivaled color. It is an ongoing legacy to which we add 30 additional projects. From cabled hats and lush blankets, to unique modular motifs and vivacious shawls, to an oversized pullover overflowing with texture and tidy cowls, this collection offers diverse and beautiful knits that are elevated by Kureyon's color magic. So, here's to an additional 30 years of knitting with Noro Kureyon. The future has never been more colorful.

The Projects

Tokyo Pullover

Tokyo Pullover

Designed by Aviva Susser

Knit from side to side, a classic sweater shape is modernized with a playful texture along the shoulders and sleeve cuffs.

Skill Level
■■■□

Sizes
Instructions are written for sizes Small (Medium, Large, X-Large). Shown in size Small.

Knitted Measurements
Bust 44 (48, 52, 56)"/111.5 (122, 132, 142)cm
Front Length (including shoulder insert) 24 (25, 26, 27)"/61 (63.5, 66, 68.5)cm
Back Length (including shoulder insert) 27¼ (28¼ , 29¼ , 30¼)"/69 (72, 74.5, 77)cm

Materials
- 12 (13, 15, 17) 1¾oz/50g skeins (each approx 110yd/100m) of Noro *Kureyon* (wool) in #332 Lime/Olive/Jade/Purple ④
- One pair size 8 (5mm) needles, *OR SIZE TO OBTAIN GAUGE*
- One size 8 (5mm) circular needle, 24"/60cm long
- Stitch markers

Gauge
15½ sts and 23 rows to 4"/10cm over St st using size 8 (5mm) needles.
TAKE TIME TO CHECK GAUGE.

Welted Ridge Pattern Stitch
Row 1 (RS) Purl.
Row 2 Knit.
Row 3 Purl.
Row 4 Purl.
Row 5 Knit.
Row 6 Purl.
Rep rows 1–6 for welted ridge pat st.

Notes
1) The front and back are worked separately from side seam to side seam.
2) Stitches for the sleeves are picked up along the side edge and worked down to the cuff.
3) Lower edge borders on front and back are picked up and worked down in finishing. The schematic lengths do not reflect this edge.

Front
With straight needles, cast on 80 (84, 88, 92) sts.

SHAPE LEFT SHOULDER
Beg with a WS row, work in St st (k on RS, p on WS) for 3 (5, 9, 11) rows.
Inc row (RS) K2, M1, k to end—1 st inc'd.
Rep inc row every 4th row 9 times more—90 (94, 98, 102) sts.
Cont even until piece measures 8¼ (9, 9¾, 10½)"/21 (23, 24.5, 26.5)cm, end with a WS row.

SHAPE NECK
Next row (RS) Bind off 13 (14, 15, 16) sts, k to end—77 (80, 83, 86) sts.
Work 1 row even.
Next row Bind off 2 sts, k to end—75 (78, 81, 84) sts.
Work 3 rows even.
Next row Bind off 2 sts, k to end—73 (76, 79, 82) sts.
Cont even for 17 (21, 23, 27) rows, end with a WS row.
Next row Cast on 2 sts, k to end—75 (78, 81, 84) sts.
Work 3 rows even.
Next row Cast on 2 sts, k to end—77 (80, 83, 86) sts.
Work 1 row even.
Next row Cast on 13 (14, 15, 16) sts, k to end—90 (94, 98, 102) sts.

SHAPE RIGHT SHOULDER
Work 5 (7, 7, 9) rows even, end with a WS row.
Dec row (RS) K2, k2tog, k to end—1 st dec'd.
Rep dec row every 4th row 9 times more—80 (84, 88, 92) sts.
Cont even until you have worked the same number of rows from neck as the first half of shoulder. Bind off.

Back

With straight needles, cast on 80 (84, 88, 92) sts.
Beg with a WS row, work in St st for 3 rows.

SHAPE RIGHT SHOULDER AND HEM

Inc row 1 (RS) K2, M1, k to last 2 sts, M1, k2—1 st inc'd at shoulder and 1 st inc'd at hem.
Rep shoulder inc (beg of RS rows) every 4th row 9 times, AT THE SAME TIME, rep hem inc (end of RS rows) every other row 6 times, then every 4th row 6 times—103 (107, 111, 115) sts.
Cont even until piece measures 8¼ (9, 9¾, 10½)"/21 (23, 24.5, 26.5)cm, end with a WS row.

SHAPE NECK

Next row (RS) Bind off 3 sts, k to end of row—100 (104, 108, 112) sts.
Work 1 row even.
Dec row K2, ssk, k to end—1 st dec'd.
Rep last 2 rows once more—98 (102, 106, 110) sts.
Cont even for 21 (25, 27, 31) rows, end with a WS row.
Inc row (RS) K2, M1, k to end—1 st inc'd.
Work 1 row even.
Rep last 2 rows once more—100 (104, 108, 112) sts.
Next row (RS) Cast on 3 sts, k to end—103 (107, 111, 115) sts.

SHAPE LEFT SHOULDER AND HEM

Work even for 7 (5, 9, 7) rows, end with a WS row.
Dec row 1 (RS) K2, ssk, k to last 4 sts, k2tog, k2—1 st dec'd at shoulder and at hem.
Rep shoulder dec (beg of RS rows) every 4th row 9 times, AT THE SAME TIME, rep hem dec (end of RS rows) every 4th row 6 times, then every other row 6 times—80 (84, 88, 92) sts.
Cont even until you have worked the same number of rows from neck as the first half of shoulder. Bind off.

Shoulder Inserts (make 2)

With straight needles, cast on 7 sts.
Beg with a RS row, work in St st for 4 rows.
Work in welted ridge pat st until piece measures to fit along one shoulder edge. Bind off.
Sew shoulder insert to each front and back shoulder.

Sleeves

Place marker each side of front and back, 7 (7½, 8, 8½)"/18 (19, 20.5, 21.5)cm from center of shoulder insert.
With straight needles and RS facing, pick up and k 54 (58, 62, 66) sts between markers.
Beg with a WS row, work even in St st for 6"/15cm, end with a WS row.
Dec row (RS) K2, ssk, k to last 4 sts, k2tog, k2—2 sts dec'd.
Rep dec row every 8th (6th, 6th, 6th) row 5 (11, 12, 12) times more, then every 6th (0, 0, 0) row 5 (0, 0, 0) times—32 (34, 36, 40) sts, AT THE SAME TIME, when sleeve measures 12"/30.5cm, end with a WS row. Work welted ridge pat st for 57 rows. **Note** If a dec row falls on a RS purl row, work ssp at beg of row and p2tog at end of row.
Bind off. Rep for other sleeve.

Finishing

Sew side and sleeve seams. If desired, leave a 2"/5cm hole for thumbs approx 2"/5cm from sleeve cuff.

NECKBAND

With circular needle and RS facing, pick up and k 90 (94, 100, 104) sts evenly along neck edge. Join to work in rnds and pm to mark beg of rnd. Knit 1 rnd. Purl 3 rnds. Bind off purlwise.

LOWER EDGE

With circular needle and RS facing, pick up and k 197 (215, 233, 251) sts along lower edge. Join to work in rnds and pm to mark beg of rnd. Knit 1 rnd. Purl 3 rnds. Bind off purlwise.
Weave in ends. Block to measurements. ❖

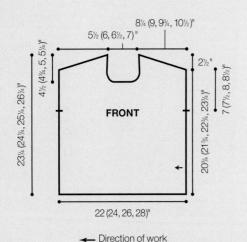

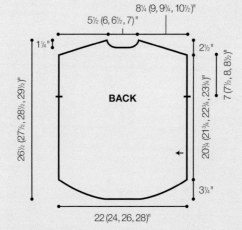

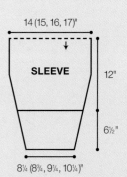

← Direction of work

– Place marker

Cable News

Cable News

Designed by Anne Jones

Cables that divide and interlace against a striped backdrop decrease in the round and culminate with a joyful burst of a pompom.

Skill Level
■■■□

Knitted Measurements
Circumference 20"/51cm
Height 11"/28cm

Materials
■ 2 1¾oz/50g skeins (each approx 110yd/100m) of Noro *Kureyon* (wool) in #359 Blues/Lilac/Yellow
■ One each sizes 8 and 9 (5 and 5.5mm) circular needles, 16"/40cm long, *OR SIZE TO OBTAIN GAUGE*
■ One set (5) size 9 (5.5mm) double-pointed needles (dpn)
■ 4 stitch markers, 1 in a different color for beg of rnd
■ Cable needle (cn)
■ One large pompom maker

Gauge
23½ sts and 24 rows to 4"/10cm over cable pat using larger needle.
TAKE TIME TO CHECK GAUGE.

Stitch Glossary
3-st RPC Sl 1 st to cn and hold to *back*, k2, p1 from cn.
3-st LPC Sl 2 sts to cn and hold to *front*, p1, k2 from cn.
4-st RC Sl 2 sts to cn and hold to *back*, k2, k2 from cn.
4-st LC Sl 2 sts to cn and hold to *front*, k2, k2 from cn.
4-st RPC Sl 2 sts to cn and hold to *back*, k2, p2 from cn.
4-st LPC Sl 2 sts to cn and hold to *front*, p2, k2 from cn.
5-st RC Sl 3 sts to cn and hold to *back*, k2, k3 from cn.
5-st LC Sl 2 sts to cn and hold to *front*, k3, k2 from cn.
5-st RPC Sl 3 sts to cn and hold to *back*, k2, p3 from cn.
5-st LPC Sl 2 sts to cn and hold to *front*, p3, k2 from cn.

Hat
With smaller circular needle, cast on 100 sts. Join to work in rnds, taking care not to twist sts on needle, and pm to mark beg of rnd.
Rnd 1 *K2, p2; rep from * around.
Rep rnd 1 for k2, p2 rib until piece measures 3½"/9cm from beg, inc 12 sts evenly around on last rnd—112 sts.
Change to larger circular needle.

BEGIN CHART
Note Change to dpn, dividing sts evenly over 4 needles, when there are too few sts to fit comfortably on circular needle.
Set-up rnd *Work rnd 1 of chart over 28 sts, pm; rep from * twice more, then work chart over rem 28 sts.
Work rnds 2–45 of chart—8 sts.
Cut yarn, leaving a long end. Pull tail through sts on needles and draw up tightly to close.

Finishing
Weave in ends. Block to measurements.
Make pompom and secure to top of hat. ❖

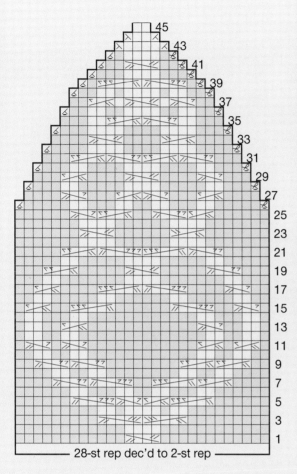

45
43
41
39
37
35
33
31
29
27
25
23
21
19
17
15
13
11
9
7
5
3
1

28-st rep dec'd to 2-st rep

STITCH KEY

□	k	4-st RC
□	p	4-st LC
p2tog		4-st RPC
p2tog tbl		4-st LPC
ssk		5-st RC
k2tog		5-st LC
3-st RPC		5-st RPC
3-st LPC		5-st LPC

Seashell Ripple

Seashell Ripple

Designed by Susan Ashcroft

An easy lace pattern creates ripples of color that culminate in a gently scalloped lower edge for a bright, reversible shawl perfect for many occasions.

Skill Level
■■□□

Knitted Measurements
Width 72"/183cm
Length 23½"/59.5cm

Materials
■ 6 1¾oz/50g skeins (each approx 110yd/100m) of Noro *Kureyon* (wool) in #326 Fuchsia/Brown/Turquoise/Blue (4)
■ One size 10 (6mm) circular needle, 32"/80cm long, *OR SIZE TO OBTAIN GAUGE*
■ One size J/10 (6mm) crochet hook
■ Stitch markers
■ Scrap yarn

Gauge
14 sts and 22 rows to 4"/10cm over St st using size 10 (6mm) needle. *TAKE TIME TO CHECK GAUGE.*

Notes
1) Shawl is worked from the top down, increasing stitches every row.
2) Slip markers as you come to them unless instructed otherwise.
3) Circular needle is used to accomodate large number of stitches. Do *not* join.

Shawl
GARTER TAB
Using provisional cast-on (see page 142), cast on 3 sts.
Knit 26 rows—13 garter ridges.

SET-UP ROWS
Next row (RS) K3, pick up and k 12 sts evenly along side edge, remove scrap yarn from provisional cast-on and k3 from cast-on edge—18 sts.
Next row K3, p to last 3 sts, k3.
Row 1 (RS) K4, [yo, k1] 5 times, pm, [yo, k1] 5 times, k4—28 sts.
Row 2 K3, yo, p to last 3 sts, yo, k3—30 sts.
Row 3 K3, yo, pm, k12, sm, k12, pm, yo, k3—32 sts.
Row 4 K3, yo, p1, sm, p to last marker, sm, p1, yo, k3—34 sts.
Row 5 K3, yo, k2, *sm, SK2P, k4, yo, k1, yo, k4; rep from * to last 5 sts, sm, k2, yo, k3—36 sts.
Row 6 K3, yo, p3, *sm, p3tog, p4, yo, p1, yo, p4; rep from * to last 6 sts, sm, p3, yo, k3—38 sts.
Row 7 K3, yo, p4, *sm, p3tog, p4, yo, p1, yo, p4; rep from * to last 7 sts, sm, p4, yo, k3—40 sts.
Row 8 K3, yo, k5, *sm, SK2P, k4, yo, k1, yo, k4; rep from * to last 8 sts, sm, k5, yo, k3—42 sts.
Row 9 K3, yo, p6, *sm, p3tog, p4, yo, p1, yo, p4; rep from * to last 9 sts, sm, p6, yo, k3—44 sts.
Row 10 K3, yo, k1, [yo, k2tog] 3 times, sm, *[yo, k1] 6 times, pm (or sm already there); rep from * to last 10 sts, sm, [yo, k2tog] 3 times, k1, yo, k3—70 sts.

LACE SECTION
Note 2 sts are inc'd on each row of next section.
Row 11 (RS) K3, yo, p to last 3 sts, yo, k3.
Row 12 K3, yo, k to last 3 sts, yo, k3.
Row 13 K3, yo, p to last 3 sts, yo, k3.
Row 14 K3, yo, k11, *sm, SK2P, k4, yo, k1, yo, k4; rep from * to last 14 sts, sm, k11, yo, k3.
Row 15 K3, yo, *pm, p3tog, p4, yo, p1, yo, p4; rep from * to last 3 sts, pm, yo, k3.
Row 16 K3, yo, p1, *sm, p3tog, p4, yo, p1, yo, p4; rep from * to last 4 sts, sm, p1, yo, k3.
Row 17 K3, yo, k2, *sm, SK2P, k4, yo, k1, yo, k4; rep from * to last 5 sts, sm, k2, yo, k3.
Row 18 K3, yo, p3, *sm, p3tog, p4, yo, p1, yo, p4; rep from * to last 6 sts, sm, p3, yo, k3.
Row 19 K3, yo, k2, yo, k2tog, sm, *yo, k2tog; rep from * to last 7 sts, sm, yo, k2tog, k2, yo, k3.
Row 20 K3, yo, p to last 3 sts, yo, k3.

Row 21 K3, yo, k to last 3 sts, yo, k3.

Row 22 K3, yo, p to last 3 sts, yo, k3.

Row 23 K3, yo, k8, *sm, SK2P, k4, yo, k1, yo, k4; rep from * to last 11 sts, sm, k8, yo, k3.

Row 24 K3, yo, k9, *sm, p3tog, p4, yo, p1, yo, p4; rep from * to last 12 sts, sm, p9, yo, k3.

Row 25 K3, yo, p10, *sm, p3tog, p4, yo, p1, yo, p4; rep from * to last 13 sts, sm, p10, yo, k3.

Row 26 K3, yo, k11, *sm, SK2P, k4, yo, k1, yo, k4; rep from * to last 14 sts, sm, k11, yo, k3.

Row 27 K3, yo, pm, *p3tog, p4, yo, p1, yo, p4; rep from * to last 3 sts, pm, yo, k3.

Row 28 K3, yo, k1, sm, *yo, k2tog; rep from * to last 4 sts, sm, k1, yo, k3.

Row 29 K3, yo, p to last 3 sts, yo, k3.

Row 30 K3, yo, k to last 3 sts, yo, k3.

Row 31 K3, yo, p to last 3 sts, yo, k3.

Row 32 K3, yo, k5, *sm, SK2P, k4, yo, k1, yo, k4; rep from * to last 8 sts, sm, k5, yo, k3.

Row 33 K3, yo, p6, *sm, p3tog, p4, yo, p1, yo, p4; rep from * to last 9 sts, sm, p6, yo, k3.

Row 34 K3, yo, p7, *sm, p3tog, p4, yo, p1, yo, p4; rep from * to last 10 sts, sm, p7, yo, k3.

Row 35 K3, yo, k8, *sm, SK2P, k4, yo, k1, yo, k4; rep from * to last 11 sts, sm, k8, yo, k3.

Row 36 K3, yo, p9, *sm, p3tog, p4, yo, p1, yo, p4; rep from * to last 12 sts, sm, p9, yo, k3.

Row 37 K3, yo, k2, *yo, k2tog; rep from * to last 5 sts, k2, yo, k3.

Row 38 K3, yo, p to last 3 sts, yo, k3.

Row 39 K3, yo, pm, k to last 3 sts, pm, yo, k3.

Row 40 K3, yo, p1, sm, p to last 4 sts, sm, p1, yo, k3.

Row 41 K3, yo, k2, *sm, SK2P, k4, yo, k1, yo, k4; rep from * to last 5 sts, sm, k2, yo, k3.

Row 42 K3, yo, p3, *sm, p3tog, p4, yo, p1, yo, p4; rep from * to last 6 sts, sm, p3, yo, k3.

Row 43 K3, yo, p4, *sm, p3tog, p4, yo, p1, yo, p4; rep from * to last 7 sts, sm, p4, yo, k3.

Row 44 K3, yo, k5, *sm, SK2P, k4, yo, k1, yo, k4; rep from * to last 8 sts, sm, k5, yo, k3.

Row 45 K3, yo, p6, *sm, p3tog, p4, yo, p1, yo, p4; rep from * to last 9 sts, sm, p6, yo, k3.

Row 46 K3, yo, k1, *yo, k2tog; rep from * to last 4 sts, k1, yo, k3.

Rep rows 11–46 once more, then rep rows 11–18 again—230 sts.

BORDER

Row 1 (RS) K3, yo, k1 tbl, k to last 4 sts, k1 tbl, yo, k3—232 sts.

Row 2 K3, yo, k1 tbl, k to marker, *sm, k5, [yo, k1] twice, yo, k5; rep from * last marker, sm, k to last 4 sts, k1 tbl, yo, k3—288 sts.

Row 3 K3, yo, k to last 3 sts, working all yo tbl, yo, k3—290 sts.

Bind off all sts loosely knitwise, working all yo tbl.

Finishing

Weave in ends. Block to measurements. ❧

Color Vine Cardigan

Color Vine Cardigan

Designed by Carolyn Noyes

The casual silhouette of a sleek cardigan provides nice contrast to a colorful woven design played out against a rich charcoal backdrop.

Skill Level
■■■■

Sizes
Instructions are written for sizes Small (Medium, Large, X-Large). Shown in size Small.

Knitted Measurements
Bust (closed) 38 (41, 44, 47)"/96.5 (104, 111.5, 119)cm
Length 24 (25, 26, 27)"/61 (63.5, 66, 68.5)cm
Upper arm 11 (12, 13, 14)"/28 (30.5, 33, 35.5)cm

Materials
■ 8 (9, 10, 12) 1¾oz/50g skeins (each approx 110yd/100m) of Noro *Silk Garden Solo* (silk/mohair/wool) in #9 Charcoal (MC) (④)
■ 4 (5, 5, 6) 1¾oz/50g skeins (each approx 110yd/100m) of Noro *Kureyon* (wool) in #188 Moss/Purples/Navy/Black/Grey (CC) (④)
■ One pair each sizes 6 and 7 (4 and 4.5mm) needles, *OR SIZE TO OBTAIN GAUGES*
■ One each sizes 6 and 7 (4 and 4.5mm) circular needle, each 24"/60cm long

■ Stitch markers
■ Stitch holders
■ One 1¾"/44mm button
■ One large snap closure

Gauges
20 sts and 36 rows to 4"/10cm over chart pat using larger needles.
21 sts and 28 rows to 4"/10cm over sl-st rib using larger needles.
TAKE TIME TO CHECK GAUGES.

Slip-Stitch Rib
(over a multiple of 5 sts)
Row 1 (RS) *Sl 1 wyib, k1, sl 1 wyib, p2; rep from * to end.
Row 2 *K2, p3; rep from * to end.
Rep rows 1 and 2 for sl-st rib.

Notes
1) Two Stockinette stitch selvage stitches are worked on every row and are not figured into the finished measurements.
2) Carry color not in use up the side of work and twist yarns tog at the beginning of row color changes.
3) Be sure to keep pattern aligned when working the shaping.

Back
With larger needles and MC, cast on 84 (89, 99, 109) sts. Purl 1 row.
Row 1 (RS) K2 (selvage sts), work row 1 of sl-st rib to last 2 sts, k2 (selvage sts).
Row 2 P2, work row 2 of sl-st rib to last 2 sts, p2.
Rep rows 1 and 2 three times more.
Next row (RS) K2, k to last 2 sts inc 18 (21, 19, 17) sts evenly spaced, k2—102 (110, 118, 126) sts. Change to CC.

BEGIN CHART
Row 1 (RS) With CC, k2 (selvage sts), work first st of chart, work 8-st rep 12 (13, 14, 15) times, work last st of chart, k2 (selvage sts).
Cont in chart pat, with 2 St st (k on RS, p on WS) selvage sts each side, until piece measures 4½"/11.5cm from beg.
Dec row (RS) K2, ssk, work to last 4 sts, k2tog, k2.
Rep dec row every 10th row twice more—96 (104, 112, 120) sts. Work even until piece measures 16½"/42cm from beg.

ARMHOLE SHAPING
Cont in pat, bind off 4 (4, 5, 5) sts at beg of next 2 rows, 2 sts at beg of next 2 rows. Dec 1 st each side every other row 1 (2, 3, 4) times—82 (88, 92, 98) sts. Work even (with 2 selvage sts on each side of rows as before), until armhole measures 6 (7, 8, 9)"/15 (18, 20.5, 23)cm.

SHOULDER SHAPING

Bind off 2 sts at beg of next 2 rows, 7 (8, 7, 8) sts at beg of next 2 rows, 6 (7, 8, 9) sts at beg of next 4 rows. Place rem 40 (40, 42, 42) sts on st holder for back neck.

Left Front

With larger needles and MC, cast on 39 (44, 49, 54) sts. Purl 1 row.
Row 1 (RS) K2 (selvage sts), work row 1 of sl-st rib to last 2 sts, k2 (selvage sts).
Row 2 P2, work row 2 of sl-st rib to last 2 sts, p2.
Rep rows 1 and 2 three times more.
Next row (RS) K2, k to last 2 sts dec'ing 1 (2, 3, 4) st(s) evenly spaced, k2—38 (42, 46, 50) sts. Change to CC.

BEGIN CHART

Row 1 (RS) With CC, k2 (selvage sts), beg with the first (5th, first, 5th) st of chart, work to rep line, work 8-st rep 4 (4, 5, 5) times, work last st of chart, k2 (selvage sts).
Cont in chart pat, with 2 St st selvage sts each side, until piece measures 4½"/11.5cm from beg.
Dec row (RS) K2, ssk, work to end.
Cont in chart pat, rep dec row every 10th row twice more—35 (39, 43, 47) sts. Work even until piece measures 16½"/42cm from beg.

ARMHOLE SHAPING

Bind off 4 (4, 5, 5) sts at beg of next RS row, then 2 sts at beg of next RS row. Dec 1 st at armhole edge on next RS row then every other row 0 (1, 2, 3) time(s) more—28 (31, 33, 36) sts. Work even until armhole measures 3¼ (4¼, 5¼, 6¼)"/8.5 (11, 13.5, 16)cm, end with a RS row.

NECK SHAPING

Next row (WS) Bind off 2 sts, work to end.
Cont to shape neck, binding off 3 (3, 4, 4) sts from neck edge once, then 2 sts once—21 (24, 25, 28) sts. Work even until armhole measures same as back.

SHOULDER SHAPING

Bind off 2 sts from shoulder edge once, 7 (8, 7, 8) sts once, 6 (7, 8, 9) sts twice.

Right Front

Cast on and work as for left front up to chart pat.

BEGIN CHART

Row 1 (RS) With CC, k2 (selvage sts), work first st of chart, work 8-st rep 4 (4, 5, 5) times, work first 1 (5, 1, 5) st(s) of rep once more, k2 (selvage sts).
Complete to correspond to left front, reversing all shaping.

Front Bands

With larger circular needle, MC, and RS facing, pick up and k 80 (84, 87, 91) sts evenly along center right front edge in between the 2 selvage sts, leaving a long end at lower edge for later use.
Purl 1 row and leave these sts on hold on circular needle.
With long end that was left at lower edge, cast on 15 sts onto one larger straight needle.
Set-up row (RS) P1, k3, p2, k3, p2, k3, then p the last st on straight needle tog with 1 st from circular needle, turn.
Next row (WS) K1, p3, k2, p3, k2, p3, k1.
Next row (RS) P1, [sl 1, k1, sl 1, p2] twice, sl 1, k1, sl 1, p last st on needle tog with 1 st from circular needle, turn.
Cont to work in this way until all sts on circular needle are joined to front band sts on larger needle. Leave 15 sts on hold at neck edge.
Work left front band in same way, only k last st on needle tog with 1 st from circular needle on WS, not RS, rows.
Leave 15 sts on hold at neck edge.

Sleeves

With larger needles and MC, cast on 50 (50, 60, 60) sts. Purl 1 row.
Next row (RS) P1 (selvage st), work 5-st rep of sl-st rib to last 4 sts, sl 1 wyib, k1, sl 1 wyib, p1 (selvage st).
Cont in sl-st rib until piece measures 2½"/6.5cm from beg, then work as foll:
Inc row (RS) P1, M1 st in pat, work to last st, M1 st in pat, p1—2 sts inc'd.
Rep inc row every 14th (8th, 14th, 8th) row 3 (5, 3, 5) times more—58 (62, 68, 72) sts.
Work even until piece measures 13"/33cm from beg.

CAP SHAPING

Bind off 4 (4, 5, 5) sts at beg of next 2 rows, 2 sts at beg of next 2 rows, 1 st at beg of next 2 rows. Dec 1 st each side of next row then every other row 12 (14, 16, 18) times more. Bind off 4 sts at beg of next 2 rows—10 sts. Work even on these 10 sts for saddle shoulders for approx 3½ (4, 4¼, 4¾)"/9 (10, 11, 12)cm or to fit across top of shoulder. Sl these sts to a holder for finishing later.

Finishing

Block pieces lightly to measurements. Sew saddle shoulder extensions across top of shoulders. Set sleeves into armholes. Sew side and sleeve seams.

NECKBAND

With smaller circular needle and MC, sl 15 sts from right front holder to needle, pick up and k 20 (20, 21, 21) sts along right front, cut yarn; sl 10 saddle shoulder sts, 40 (40, 42, 42) sts from back neck, 10 saddle shoulder sts to needle, pick up and k 20 (20, 22, 22) sts along left front, cut yarn; sl 15 sts from left front holder to needle—130 (130, 135, 135) sts.
Row 1 (RS) With MC, p1, work sl-st rib to last 2 sts, sl 1 wyib, p1.
Cont in sl-st rib pat for 2"/5cm. Bind off, working p2tog over each p2 rib.
Sew on snap 1"/2.5cm from top neck edge and 1"/2.5cm in from center. Sew button on top of right front snap. ❖

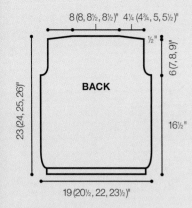

BACK

8 (8, 8½, 8½)"   4¼ (4¾, 5, 5½)"

½"

6 (7, 8, 9)"

23 (24, 25, 26)"

16½"

19 (20½, 22, 23½)"

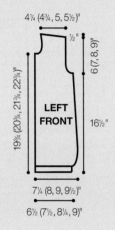

4¼ (4¾, 5, 5½)"

½"

6 (7, 8, 9)"

LEFT FRONT

19¾ (20¾, 21¾, 22¾)"

16½"

7¼ (8, 9, 9½)"

6½ (7½, 8¼, 9)"

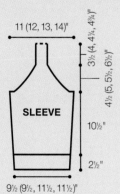

SLEEVE

11 (12, 13, 14)"

3½ (4, 4¼, 4¾)"

4½ (5, 5½, 6½)"

10½"

2½"

9½ (9½, 11½, 11½)"

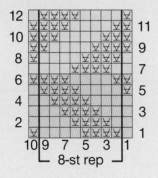

12 10 8 6 4 2
11 9 7 5 3 1

10 9 7 5 3 1

8-st rep

STITCH KEY

☐ k on RS, p on WS

Ⅴ slip 1 wyif on RS, slip 1 wyib on WS

COLOR KEY

☐ MC

▨ CC

Water Lilies

Water Lilies

Designed by Irina Poludnenko

Short rows and picked-up stitches form the 20 sewn-together squares, creating a stunning piece that calls to mind Monet's garden at Giverny.

Skill Level
■■■□

Knitted Measurements
Length 45"/114.5cm
Width 36"/99cm

Materials
- 8 1¾oz/50g skeins (each approx 110yd/100m) of Noro *Kureyon* (wool) in #359 Blues/Lilac/Yellow (A) (**4**)
- 7 skeins in #40 Aqua/Purple Multi (B)
- One pair size 9 (5.5mm) needles, *OR SIZE TO OBTAIN GAUGE*
- One size 9 (5.5mm) circular needle, 32"/80cm long
- One set (5) size 9 (5.5mm) double-pointed needles (dpn)
- Stitch markers

Gauge
16 sts and 32 rows to 4"/10cm over garter st using size 9 (5.5mm) needles.
TAKE TIME TO CHECK GAUGE.

Note
See page 142 for instructions on how to work short row wrap & turn (w&t).

Water Lily (make 20)
LILY CENTER
With straight needles and A, cast on 14 sts.
***Next row (WS)** Knit over all sts.
Short rows 1 and 2 K12, w&t, k to end of row.
Short rows 3 and 4 K11, w&t, k to end of row.
Cont in this manner, reducing 1 st before each w&t.
Short rows 23 and 24 K1, w&t, k to end of row.
Knit 1 row over all sts.
Rep from * 5 times more. Bind off all sts knitwise.
Sew tog cast-on and bound-off edges. Lily center is complete.

WATER CORNERS
Join B to lily center at seam. With RS facing and dpn, pick up and k 104 sts around entire outer edge of piece, dividing sts evenly over 4 needles—26 sts on each dpn. Place marker and join to work in the rnd. Purl one rnd.
**Work back and forth in rows over 26 sts on one dpn as foll:
Next row (RS) K1, ssk, k to last 3 sts, k2tog, k1—24 sts.
Short rows 1 and 2 K5, w&t, k2, k2tog, k1.
Short rows 3 and 4 K7, w&t, k4, k2tog, k1.
Next row (WS) K to end of dpn.
Short rows 5 and 6 K1, ssk, k2, w&t, k4.
Short rows 7 and 8 K1, ssk, k4, w&t, k6—20 sts.
Next row (RS) K1, ssk, k to last 3 sts, k2tog, k1—2 sts dec'd.
Next row (WS) K to end of dpn.
Rep last two rows until 4 sts rem on dpn, end with a RS row.
Next row (WS) K1, k2tog, k1—3 sts.
Next row K3tog. Fasten off last st.
Rep from ** 3 times more to complete each rem corner.
One water lily is now complete.

Finishing
Weave in ends. Block each water lily blanket square to 10"/25.5cm square. Assemble water lilies into a 5 by 4 grid and seam tog with B, making sure corners line up.
With RS facing, A, and circular needle, pick up and k 170 sts evenly along one long edge of blanket for border. Knit 1 row, then bind off all sts knitwise, do *not* cut yarn.
Beg in bound-off row of previous border, pick up and k 138 sts evenly along adjacent short edge, work as previous border.
Beg in bound-off row of previous border, pick up and k 172 sts evenly along adjacent long edge, work as previous border.
Beg in bound-off row of previous border, pick up and k 140 sts evenly along rem short edge, work as previous border. Fasten off last st. Weave in rem ends. ❖

Winter Brocade Hooded Scarf

Winter Brocade Hooded Scarf

Designed by Ellen Liguori

Highly textured Guernsey brocade combines with an elfin hooded scarf for a delightful twist on keeping warm.

Skill Level
■■□□

Knitted Measurements
Length 71½"/181.5cm
Width 10"/25.5cm

Materials
■ 6 1¾oz/50g skeins (each approx 110yd/100m) of Noro *Kureyon* (wool) in #359 Blues/Lilac/Yellow **④**
■ One pair size 8 (5mm) needles, *OR SIZE TO OBTAIN GAUGE*
■ Removable stitch markers

Gauge
18 sts and 30 rows to 4"/10cm over winter brocade pat on size 8 (5mm) needles.
TAKE TIME TO CHECK GAUGE.

Winter Brocade Pattern
(multiple of 18 sts)
Row 1 (RS) *K1, p2, k3, p2, k5, p1, k4; rep from * to end.
Row 2 *P3, k1, p1, k1, p3, k2, p5, k2; rep from * to end.
Row 3 *K1, [p2, k3] twice, [p1, k1] twice, p1, k2; rep from * to end.
Row 4 *P3, k1, p1, k1, p5, k2, p1, k2, p2; rep from * to end.
Row 5 *K3, p1, k1, p1, k5, [p1, k1] twice, p1, k2; rep from * to end.
Row 6 *[P1, k1] 4 times, p3, k2, p1, k2, p2; rep from * to end.
Row 7 *K1, p2, k3, p2, [k1, p1] 5 times; rep from * to end.
Row 8 *[P1, k1] 4 times, p1, k2, p5, k2; rep from * to end.
Row 9 *K1, p2, k3, p2, k10; rep from* to end.
Row 10 *K9, p2, k2, p1, k2, p2; rep from* to end.
Row 11 *K3, p1, k1, p1, k12; rep from * to end.
Row 12 *K9, p2, k2, p1, k2, p2; rep from * to end.
Rep rows 1–12 for winter brocade pat.

Note
Brocade pattern can be worked from chart or written instructions.

Scarf
RIGHT HALF
Cast on 46 sts.
Knit 7 rows.
Next row (RS) K5, pm, work row 1 of winter brocade pat over 36 sts, pm, k5.
Next row (WS) K5, sm, work row 2 of winter brocade pat over 36 sts, sm, k5.
Cont in pat until piece measures 29"/73.5cm from beg, end with a RS row.

SHAPE HOOD
Dec row (WS) Ssk, k3, sm, work next row of winter brocade pat over 36 sts, sm, k5—45 sts.
Next row (RS) K5, sm, work next row of winter brocade pat over 36 sts, sm, k4.
Dec row Ssk, k2, sm, work next row of winter brocade pat over 36 sts, sm, k5—44 sts.
Place marker on st at beg of last row.

Work even in pat for 6"/15cm, end with a RS row.

Next row (WS) Sl 1, work in pat to end.

Next row Work in pat to last 2 sts, sl 2.

Next row Sl 3, work in pat to end.

Next row Work in pat to last 2 sts, sl 2.

Next row Sl 1, work in pat to end.

Work even for 6"/15cm, end with a RS row.

Place marker on st at beg of last row.

Inc row (WS) K1, M1, work in pat to end—45 sts.

Next row Work in pat to last 4 sts, k4.

Inc row K1, M1, work in pat to end—46 sts.

LEFT HALF

Next row (RS) Work in established pat to last 5 sts, sm, k5.

Cont even in pat until left side measures 28"/71cm from last marker, end with a WS row.

Knit 7 rows.

Bind off.

Finishing

Weave in ends. Block to measurements. Fold scarf in half with RS held tog and match markers. Sew shaped edges tog from markers to fold. ✤

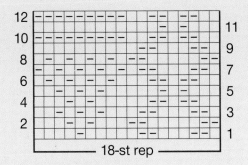

18-st rep

STITCH KEY

☐ k on RS, p on WS

⊟ p on RS, k on WS

Refined Stripes Cardigan

Refined Stripes Cardigan

Designed by Jacqueline van Dillen

Infuse garter stitch with vibrant color and bend it around your shoulders and waist with a thrilling and unconventional cardigan construction.

Skill Level
■■■□

Sizes
Instructions are written for sizes Small (Medium, Large, X-Large). Shown in size Small.

Knitted Measurements
Bust (closed) 42 (44, 46, 48)"/106.5 (111.5, 117, 122)cm
Length 21 (21½, 22, 22½)"/53 (54.5, 56, 57)cm
Upper arm 14½ (15½, 16½, 17½)"/37 (39.5, 42, 44.5)cm

Materials
- 11 (12, 13, 14) 1¾oz/50g skeins (each approx 110yd/100m) of Noro *Kureyon* (wool) in #388 West Winds (**4**)
- One pair size 8 (5mm) needles, *OR SIZE TO OBTAIN GAUGE*
- One size 8 (5mm) circular needle, 24"/60cm long
- Removable stitch markers
- Stitch holders
- One hook and eye closure

Gauge
15 sts and 30 rows to 4"/10cm over garter st using size 8 (5mm) needles. *TAKE TIME TO CHECK GAUGE.*

Notes
1) Cardigan is constructed by working from one sleeve cuff edge to opposite sleeve cuff edge for the upper piece. The lower edge is then worked by picking up stitches along the lower edge of the first piece and working down to the hem.
2) Circular needle is used to accommodate large number of stitches. Do *not* join.

Upper Piece
With straight needles, cast on 36 (40, 44, 48) sts for left sleeve cuff edge. Work 8 rows in garter st (k every row).
Inc row Kfb, k to last 2 sts, kfb, k1.
Rep inc row every 8th row 8 times more—54 (58, 62, 66) sts. Work even until piece measures 12"/30.5cm from beg.

ARMHOLE AND SLEEVE SHAPING
Cast on 2 sts at beg of next 4 rows, then cast on 17 sts at beg of next 2 rows—96 (100, 104, 108) sts. Work even for 6½ (7, 7½, 8)"/16.5 (18, 19, 20.5)cm more, end with a WS row.

SEPARATE FOR BACK AND FRONT
Next row (RS) K48 (50, 52, 54) for back, sl rem 48 (50, 52, 54) sts to circular needle to be worked later for left front.
Work even on back sts for 60 rows or 8"/20.5cm for back neck. Place sts on st holder.

LEFT FRONT
Work this section on circular needle in rows. Do *not* join.
Return to 48 (50, 52, 54) sts on hold for left front and join yarn to work a RS row.
Next row (RS) Cast on 15 sts (for one half of shawl collar to fit to center back of neck), k to end—63 (65, 67, 69) sts.
Knit 27 rows. Bind off. This is the center left front edge.

RIGHT FRONT
Note Create a separate piece that will be joined to upper piece to complete right front and right sleeve.
With circular needle, cast on 63 (65, 67, 69) sts. Do *not* join. Work back and forth in rows. Knit 28 rows.

Next row (RS) Bind off 15 sts. Cut yarn.

Place 48 (50, 52, 54) sts from back onto circular needle in front of current sts. Join yarn to work a RS row, beg with back sts.

Next row (RS) K48 (50, 52, 54) sts from back, then k48 (50, 52, 54) sts from right front.

Cont on straight needles, work even on these 96 (100, 104, 108) sts for 6½ (7, 7½, 8)"/16.5 (18, 19, 20.5)cm more.

ARMHOLE AND SLEEVE SHAPING

Bind off 17 sts at beg of next 2 rows, bind off 2 sts at beg of next 4 rows—54 (58, 62, 66) sts. Place marker each side of last row worked. Work even for 16 rows.

Dec row (RS) K2tog, k to last 2 sts, k2tog.

Rep dec row every 8th row 8 times more—36 (40, 44, 48) sts. Work even until piece measures 12"/30.5cm from placed st markers. Bind off.

Lower Piece

Sew side and underarm sleeve seams.

With circular needle and with RS facing, pick up and k35 (37, 39, 41) sts from lower left front edge, 72 (76, 80, 84) sts from lower back edge, and 35 (37, 39, 41) sts from lower right front edge—142 (150, 158, 166) sts.

Knit 65 rows or until lower piece measures 8½"/21.5cm. Bind off.

Finishing

Place marker at center back neck on upper piece.

Sew shawl collar edges along top of back neck. Sew shawl collar seam at center back neck.

FRONT AND COLLAR BORDER

With circular needle and RS facing, pick up and k 186 (190, 194, 198) sts evenly along entire center front and neck edge. Cut yarn.

Slide first and last 46 (48, 50, 52) sts to separate needles or strands of waste yarn.

Rejoin yarn to center 94 sts to work a RS row. Work short row shaping (see page 142), adding sts from waste yarn or separate needles as foll:

Short row 1 (RS) K93, w&t, turn.

Short row 2 K96, w&t.

Short row 3 K100, w&t.

Short row 4 K104, w&t.

Short row 5 K108, w&t.

Short row 6 K112, w&t.

Short row 7 K116, w&t.

Short row 8 K120, w&t.

Short row 9 K124, w&t.

Short row 10 K to end of row.

Knit 3 rows over all 186 (190, 194, 198) sts. Bind off knitwise.

Block finished piece lightly to measurements.

Sew hook and eye closure at top of lower edge. ❖

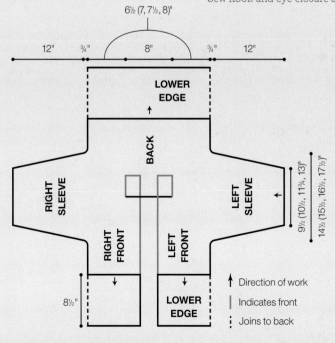

Woven Lilac Cowl

Woven Lilac Cowl

Designed by Alexandra Davidoff

Cables and lace are cleverly woven together in a doubled-up cowl embellished with I-cord and pompoms.

Skill Level

■■■□

Knitted Measurements

Circumference 21"/53.5cm
Length (with rib folded) 5"/12.5cm

Materials

- 2 1¾oz/50g skeins (each approx 110yd/100m) of Noro *Kureyon* (wool) in #188 Moss/Purples/Navy/Black/Grey (**4**)
- One size 8 (5mm) circular needle, 16"/40cm long, *OR SIZE TO OBTAIN GAUGE*
- One pair size 8 (5mm) double-pointed needles (dpn)
- Stitch marker
- Cable needle (cn)
- One small pompom maker

Gauge

19¾ sts and 21 rnds to 4"/10cm over lace cable pat using size 8 (5mm) needles.
TAKE TIME TO CHECK GAUGE.

Notes

1) Lace cable pattern can be worked from chart or written instructions.
2) As cowl is worked in the round, read each row from right to left.

Stitch Glossary

6-st RC Sl 3 sts to cn and hold to *back*, k3, k3 from cn.
6-st LC Sl 3 sts to cn and hold to *front*, k3, k3 from cn.

Lace Cable Pattern

(multiple of 17 sts)
Rnd 1 *P1, k2, yo, k4, S2KP, k4, yo, k2, p1; rep from * around.
Rnd 2 and all even-numbered rnds *P1, k15, p1; rep from * around.
Rnd 3 *P1, k3, yo, k3, S2KP, k3, yo, k3, p1; rep from * around.
Rnd 5 *P1, k4, yo, k2, S2KP, k2, yo, k4, p1; rep from * around.
Rnd 7 *P1, k5, yo, k1, S2KP, k1, yo, k5, p1; rep from * around.
Rnd 9 *P1, k6, yo, S2KP, yo, k6, p1; rep from * around.
Rnd 11 *P1, 6-st RC, yo, S2KP, yo, 6-st LC, p1; rep from * around.
Rnd 13 *P1, k6, yo, S2KP, yo, k6, p1; rep from * around.
Rnd 14 Rep rnd 2.
Rep rnds 1–14 for lace cable pat.

Cowl

With circular needle, loosely cast on 102 sts. Join, taking care not to twist sts on needle, and pm to mark beg of rnd.
Work rnds 1–14 of lace cable pat twice.
Next rnd *P1, k2, p2, k2, p3, k2, p2, k2, p1; rep from * around.
Rep last rnd until ribbing measures 4"/10cm. Bind off in pat.

Finishing

Weave in ends. Block lace cable pat to measurements.
With dpn, cast on 3 sts. Work I-cord (see page 142) for approx 13"/33cm. Bind off. Thread I-cord through 2 holes of first rep of lace cable pat rnd 13.
Make 2 small pompoms. Attach a pompom to each end of I-cord. Tie I-cord in bow. Fold ribbing to inside. ❖

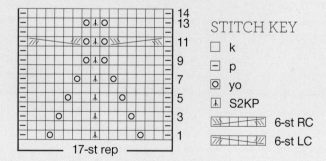

STITCH KEY
☐ k
⊟ p
⊙ yo
⋏ S2KP
6-st RC
6-st LC

17-st rep

The Electric Slip

The Electric Slip

Designed by Caroline Dick

The humble slip stitch is all you need to make the vibrant colors in a wide cowl jump as if touched by a current.

Skill Level

Knitted Measurements

Circumference 27¼"/69cm
Height 9"/23cm

Materials

■ 2 1¾oz/50g skeins (each approx 110yd/100m) of Noro *Kureyon* (wool) in #272 Reds/Purple/Mint/Yellow (❹)
■ One size 8 (5mm) circular needle, 24"/60cm long, *OR SIZE TO OBTAIN GAUGE*
■ Stitch marker

Gauge

16½ sts and 25 rnds to 4"/10cm over electric sl pat using size 8 (5mm) needle.
TAKE TIME TO CHECK GAUGE.

Electric Slip Pattern

(multiple of 8 sts plus 8)
Rnd 1 With ball B, *k4, sl 4 wyib; rep from * to last 8 sts, k4, sl 4 wyib.
Rnd 2 K5, *sl 2 wyib, k6; rep from * to last 3 sts, sl 2 wyib, k1.
Rnds 3 and 4 Knit.
Rnd 5 With ball A, *sl 4 wyib, k4; rep from * to last 8 sts, sl 4 wyib, k4.
Rnd 6 K1, *sl 2 wyib, k6; rep from * to last 7 sts, sl 2 wyib, k5.
Rnds 7 and 8 Knit.
Rep rnds 1–8 for electric sl pat.

Notes

1) Label one skein as ball A and the other as ball B. Work with both whole skeins for electric slip pattern.
2) Carry unused color loosely up along the wrong side.
3) When slipping stitches, make sure to carry the yarn loosely across the wrong side of the work.
4) Electric slip pattern can be worked from chart or written instructions.
5) As cowl is worked in the round, read each row from right to left.

Cowl

With ball A, cast on 112 sts. Join, taking care not to twist sts on needle, and pm to mark beg of rnd.
Rnds 1–8 *K2, p2; rep from * around.
Knit 2 rnds.
Join ball B. Work rnds 1–8 of electric sl pat six times. Cut ball A.
With ball B, knit 2 rnds.
Rnds 1–8 *K2, p2; rep from * around.
Bind off in pat.

Finishing

Weave in ends. Block to measurements. ♣

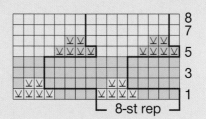

STITCH KEY
☐ k with ball A
☐ k with ball B
☑ slip 1 wyib

Diamond Spiral Cape

Diamond Spiral Cape

Designed by Jin Parker

Make a cape twice as cozy by holding two strands together and working diamond-shaped cables that encircle moss stitch sections.

Skill Level
■■■□

Knitted Measurements
Bottom circumference approx 57½"/146cm
Length 16"/40.5cm

Materials
■ 8 1¾oz/50g skeins (each approx 110yd/100m) of Noro *Kureyon* (wool) in #211 Naturals
■ One each sizes 10 and 11 (6 and 8mm) circular needles, 32"/80cm long, *OR SIZE TO OBTAIN GAUGE*
■ One pair size 10 (6mm) needles
■ Cable needle (cn)
■ Five 1"/25mm buttons
■ Contrasting scrap yarn

Gauge
9½ sts and 16 rows to 4"/10cm over cable pat using larger needles and 2 strands of yarn held tog.
TAKE TIME TO CHECK GAUGE.

Tubular Cast-on
1) With contrasting scrap yarn, cast on the required number of stitches using a backward loop cast-on. Cut the yarn.
2) With the main yarn, work as follows: k1, *yo, k1; rep from * to end of row. Turn.
3) *K1, bring yarn to front, sl next stitch purlwise, bring yarn to back; rep from* to last st, k1. Turn.
4) *Bring yarn to front, sl 1 purlwise, bring yarn to back, k1; rep from * to last stitch, bring yarn to front, sl 1 purlwise.
Cast-on is now complete. Cont in designated pat. After a few rows in pat, carefully remove the scrap yarn.

Stitch Glossary
3-st RC Sl 1 st to cn and hold to *back*, k2, k1 from cn.
3-st LC Sl 2 sts to cn and hold to *front*, k1, k2 from cn.
3-st RPC Sl 1 st to cn and hold to *back*, k2, p1 from cn.
3-st LPC Sl 2 sts to cn and hold to *front*, p1, k2 from cn.
5-st LC Sl 3 sts to cn and hold to *front*, k2, k3 from cn.

Notes
1) Cape is worked holding 2 strands of yarn together throughout.
2) Circular needle is used to accommodate large number of stitches. Do *not* join.

Body
With larger circular needle and contrasting scrap yarn, cast on 67 sts using the backward loop cast-on. With 2 strands of main yarn held tog, cont with steps 2–4 of tubular cast-on method—133 sts. Beg with row 1, work 55 rows of chart—63 sts.

NECKBAND
Change to smaller circular needle.
Dec row (RS) P2, k2, k2tog, k1, p3, k2tog, k4, p2tog, p2, k2, k2tog, k1, p3, k2tog, k4, p2tog, p2, k2, k2tog, k1, p3, k2tog, k4, p2tog, p2, k2, k2tog, k1, p2—53 sts.
Next row (WS) *P1, k1; rep from * to last st, p1.
Next row K the knit sts and p the purl sts.
Rep last row for k1, p1 rib for 4 rows more. Bind off loosely in pat.

BUTTON BAND
With straight needles, cast on 9 sts.
Row 1 (RS) K1, [k1, p1] 4 times.
Row 2 [K1, p1] 4 times, p1.
Rep rows 1 and 2 until piece measures 16"/40.5cm from beg. Bind off in pat.

BUTTONHOLE BAND
With straight needles, cast on 9 sts.
Work same as button band until piece measures approx 3"/7.5cm

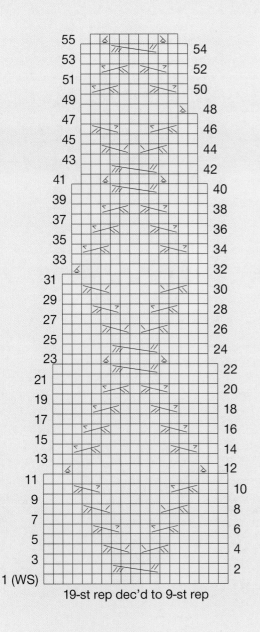

19-st rep dec'd to 9-st rep

from beg, end with a WS row.

Buttonhole row (RS) K2, p1, k1, yo, k2tog, p1, k1, p1.
Rep buttonhole row every 3"/7.5cm 4 times more. Cont in rib until piece measures 16"/40.5cm from beg. Bind off in pat.

Finishing

Weave in ends. Block to finished measurements.
Sew button band to left front. Sew buttonhole band to right front.
Sew buttons to button band opposite buttonholes. ❧

STITCH KEY

□ k on RS, p on WS	3-st LC
□ p on RS, k on WS	3-st RPC
◿ p2tog on RS, k2tog on WS	3-st LPC
◺ ssp on RS, ssk on WS	5-st LC
3-st RC	

Patchwork

Patchwork

Designed by Jill Gutman Schoenfuss

Intarsia squares shimmer down the length of a slim scarf, hemmed in by multi-colored seed stitch borders.

Skill Level
■■■□

Knitted Measurements
Width 4¾"/12cm
Length 64"/162.5cm

Materials
- 2 1¾oz/50g skeins (each approx 110yd/100m) of Noro *Kureyon* (wool) each in #388 West Winds (A) and #343 Natural/Brown/Pink/Green (B) (4)
- One pair size 8 (5mm) needles, *OR SIZE TO OBTAIN GAUGE*
- Bobbins (optional)

Gauge
16½ sts and 29 rows to 4"/10cm over St st using size 8 (5mm) needles.
TAKE TIME TO CHECK GAUGE.

Seed Stitch
(even number of sts)
Row 1 (RS) *K1, p1; rep from * to end.
Row 2 K the purl sts and p the knit sts.
Rep row 2 for seed st.

Patchwork Squares Pattern
Row 1 (RS) With B, work 4 sts in seed st; with A, k12; with B, work 4 sts in seed st.
Row 2 With B, work 4 sts in seed st; with A, p12; with B, work 4 sts in seed st.
Rows 3–6 Rep rows 1 and 2 twice more.
Row 7 With B, work 4 sts in seed st; with A, k4; with B, k4; with A, k4; with B, work 4 sts in seed st.
Row 8 With B, work 4 sts in seed st; with A, p4; with B, p4; with A, p4; with B, work 4 sts in seed st.
Rows 9–12 Rep rows 7 and 8 twice more.
Rows 13–18 Rep rows 1 and 2 three times more.
Rows 19–36 Rep rows 1–18, keeping seed st border in B but swapping A and B for center 12 sts for squares.
Rep rows 1–36 for patchwork squares pat.

Notes
1) Use a separate ball for each color section. Do *not* carry yarn across back of work.
2) When changing colors, twist yarns on WS to prevent holes in work.
3) As each skein is unique, use the chart and photo as guides to create intarsia squares with high contrast.
4) Color A is used for squares only. Color B is used for both the border and a limited number of squares. For rows 19–36, make sure B for borders and B for squares have a high contrast.
5) Patchwork squares pattern can be worked from chart or written instructions.

Scarf
Wind several bobbins or butterflies each of A and B, each with a single color of the color rep.
With B, cast on 20 sts. Work 6 rows in seed st.
Work rows 1–36 of patchwork squares pat 12 times, then work rows 1–18 once more for a total of 25 squares.
With B used for seed st border only, work 6 rows in seed st.
Bind off all sts loosely in pat.

Finishing
Weave in ends. Block to measurements. ❧

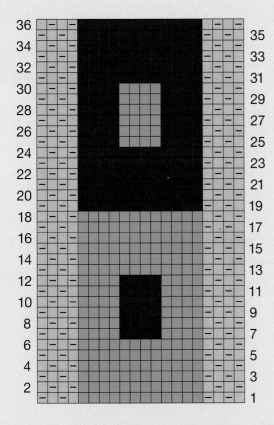

| 36 | | − | | − | | | | | | | | | | | | − | | − | | 35 |

STITCH KEY

□ k on RS, p on WS

− p on RS, k on WS

COLOR KEY

■ A   ■ B   ■ B

Castaway

Castaway

Designed by Vickie Howell

This generously sized shawl's buttonhole motif is created through a meditative series of cast-ons and bind-offs.

Skill Level
■■■□

Knitted Measurements
Width 61"/155cm
Length 42"/106.5cm

Materials
- 11 1¾oz/50g skeins (each approx 110yd/100m) of Noro *Kureyon* (wool) in #327 Violet/Blue/Turquoise/Brown
- One size 9 (5.5mm) circular needle, 32"/80cm long, *OR SIZE TO OBTAIN GAUGE*

Gauge
16 sts and 28 rows to 4"/10cm over garter st using size 9 (5.5mm) needle. *TAKE TIME TO CHECK GAUGE.*

Notes
1) Shawl is worked from the bottom up.
2) Mark the right side of the work.
3) Circular needle is used to accommodate large number of stitches. Do *not* join.
4) See page 142 for instructions on how to work short row wrap & turn (w&t).

Shawl
Cast on 5 sts.
Rows 1–6 Knit.
Rows 7 and 8 Cast on 5 sts, k to end—15 sts.
Row 9 (RS) K5, bind off 5 sts, k5.
Note After binding off sts, there is 1 st on RH needle after bound-off sts; this counts as first st of k5.
Row 10 (WS) K5, cast on 5 sts over bound-off sts, k to end—15 sts.
Rows 11–13 Knit.
Row 14 Purl.
Rows 15 and 16 Cast on 5 sts, k to end—25 sts.
Rows 17–20 Knit.
Row 21 [K5, bind off 5 sts] twice, k5.
Row 22 [K5, cast on 5 sts over bound-off sts] twice, k5—25 sts.
Rows 23–25 Knit.
Row 26 Purl.
Rows 27 and 28 Cast on 5 sts, k to end—10 sts inc'd.
Rows 29–32 Knit.
Row 33 *K5, bind off 5 sts; rep from * to last 5 sts, k5.
Row 34 *K5, cast on 5 sts over bound-off sts; rep from * to last 5 sts, k5.
Rows 35–37 Knit.
Row 38 Purl.
Rep rows 27–38 twenty times—235 sts.
Knit 4 rows.

SHORT ROW SECTION 1
Row 1 (RS) K40, w&t.
Row 2 K to end of row.
Row 3 K to 2 sts before wrapped st, w&t.
Row 4 K to end of row.
Rows 5–24 Rep rows 3 and 4 ten times more.
Row 25 K to 4 sts before wrapped st, w&t.
Row 26 K to end of row.
Rows 27–32 Rep rows 25 and 26 three times more.
Row 28 K to end of row.

SHORT ROW SECTION 2
Beg with a WS row, rep short row section 1 on opposite end.
Bind off all sts knitwise.

Finishing
Weave in ends. Block to measurements. ✤

Squared

Squared

Designed by Margie Kieper

Gradient blocks create a textile mosaic, framed by ribbed sleeves, neck, and hem.

Skill Level
■■■□

Sizes
Instructions are written for sizes Small/Medium (Large/X-Large, XX-Large). Shown in size Small/Medium.

Knitted Measurements
Bust 54 (60, 66)"/137 (152, 167.5)cm
Length 21½"/54.5cm
Upperarm 12 (14, 16)"/30.5 (35.5, 40.5)cm

Materials
- 3 (3, 4) 1¾oz/50g skeins (each approx 110yd/100m) of Noro *Kureyon* (wool) each in #40 Aqua/Purple Multi, #344 Jade/Sky/Green/Brown, #359 Blues/Lilac/Yellow, and #381 Violet's Memoir
- Two size 8 (5mm) circular needles, each 12 and 32"/30 and 82cm long, *OR SIZE TO OBTAIN GAUGE*
- Stitch markers

Gauge
15 sts and 24 rows to 4"/10cm over St st using size 8 (5mm) needle.
TAKE TIME TO CHECK GAUGE.

Notes
1) Circular needle is used to accommodate large number of sts. Do *not* join.
2) Wrap 72 (80, 88) 6yd/5.5m-lengths of yarn in preferred colors from skeins, and arrange color selection in a grid 8 high by 9 (10, 11) wide. Label each color C1, C2, C3, etc. (see placement diagram). Use remaining yarn for ribbed edges and sleeves as desired.
3) Strips of color are worked in intarsia. When changing colors, twist yarns on WS to prevent holes in work.
4) An extra selvage stitch has been added to each side of the front and back for seaming. These stitches are not counted in the finished measurements.

Back
With desired color, cast on 101 (112, 123) sts.
Row 1 (RS) *K1, p1; rep from * to end.
Rep last row for k1, p1 rib for 5 rows more, and on last WS row, dec 0 (1, 0) st(s)—101 (112, 123) sts.

BEGIN BLOCK PATTERN
Work in St st (k on RS, p on WS) as foll:

For Size Small/Medium Only
Row 1 (RS) K12 with C1, k11 sts each C2, C3, C4, C5, C6, C7, C8, k last 12 sts with C9.

For Size Large/X-Large Only
Row 1 (RS) K12 with C1, k11 sts each C2, C3, C4, C5, C6, C7, C8, C9, k last 12 sts with C10.

For Size XX-Large Only
Row 1 (RS) K12 with C1, k11 sts each C2, C3, C4, C5, C6, C7, C8, C9, C10, k last 12 sts with C11.

For All Sizes
Row 2 (WS) Purl, matching colors.
Rep rows 1 and 2 three times more (8 rows in total).
Row 9 (RS) Knit, matching all odd-numbered colors and replacing all even-numbered colors.
Rows 10–16 Cont in St st, matching colors.
Row 17 (RS) Knit, matching all even-numbered colors and replacing all odd-numbered colors.
Rows 18–24 Cont in St st, matching colors.
Cont in pat, changing colors as established or foll diagram, until 112 rows have been worked in block pat. Piece measures approx 20"/51cm from beg.

SHOULDER AND NECK SHAPING
Mark center 33 (36, 39) sts.
Row 1 (RS) Bind off 8 (9, 10) sts, work to end of row.
Row 2 Bind off 8 (9, 10) sts, work to end of row—85 (94, 103) sts.

Row 3 Bind off 8 (9, 10) sts, work to center sts, join new ball of yarn and bind off center 33 (36, 39) sts, work to end of row. Cont working each side at once, as foll:

Row 4 (WS) *First Side*: Bind off 8 (9, 10) sts, work to end. *Second Side*: Work to end—18 (20, 22) sts each side.

Row 5 *First Side*: Bind off 8 (9, 10) sts, work to end. *Second Side*: Bind off 2 sts, work to end.

Row 6 *First Side*: Bind off 8 (9, 10) sts, work to end. *Second Side*: Bind off 2 sts, work to end—8 (9, 10) sts each side.

Row 7 *First Side*: Bind off 7 (8, 9) sts, work to end. *Second Side*: Bind off 1 st, work to end.

Row 8 Bind off rem sts on each side.

Front

Work as for back until 112 rows have been worked in block pat. Piece measures approx 20"/51cm from beg.

SHOULDER AND NECK SHAPING
Mark center 27 (30, 33) sts.

Row 1 (RS) Bind off 8 (9, 10) sts, work to center sts, join new ball of yarn and bind off center 27 (30, 33) sts, work to end of row. Cont working each side at once, as foll:

Row 2 *First Side*: Bind off 8 (9, 10) sts, work to end. *Second Side*: Work to end—29 (32, 35) sts each side.

Row 3 *First Side*: Bind off 8 (9, 10) sts, work to end. *Second Side*: Bind off 2 sts, work to end.

Row 4 *First Side*: Bind off 8 (9, 10) sts, work to end. *Second Side*: Bind off 2 sts, work to end—19 (21, 23) sts each side.

Row 5 *First Side*: Bind off 8 (9, 10) sts, work to end. *Second Side*: Bind off 2 sts, work to end.

Row 6 *First Side*: Bind off off 8 (9, 10) sts, work to end. *Second Side*: Bind off 2 sts, work to end—9 (10, 11) sts each side.

Row 7 *First Side*: Bind off 7 (8, 9) sts, work to end. *Second Side*: Bind off 2 sts, work to end.

Row 8 Bind off rem sts on each side.

Sleeves (make 2)

With desired color, cast on 43 (51, 57) sts. Work in k1, p1 rib for 9"/23cm. Bind off loosely in rib.

Finishing

Block front and back pieces to measurements. Do *not* block sleeves. Sew shoulder seams. Place markers 6 (7, 8)"/15.5 (18, 20.5)cm down from shoulder seams on front and back. Sew top of sleeve (stretching to fit) between markers. Sew side and sleeve seams. Weave in ends.

NECKBAND
With RS facing and desired color, pick up and k 84 (90, 96) sts evenly around neck edge. Join to work in rnds and pm for beg of rnd. Work in k1, p1 rib for 5 rnds. Bind off loosely in rib. ❧

PLACEMENT DIAGRAM

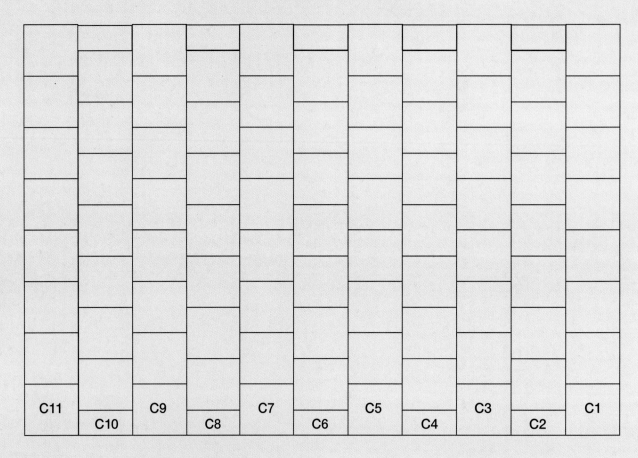

| C11 | | C9 | | C7 | | C5 | | C3 | | C1 |
| | C10 | | C8 | | C6 | | C4 | | C2 | |

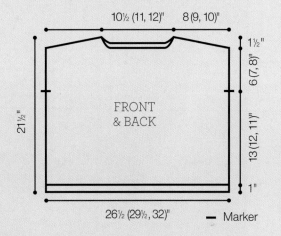

10½ (11, 12)"   8 (9, 10)"

1½"

6 (7, 8)"

21½"

FRONT
& BACK

13 (12, 11)"

1"

26½ (29½, 32)"   ▬ Marker

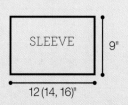

SLEEVE   9"

12 (14, 16)"

Farmhouse Felt

Farmhouse Felt

Designed by Jacqueline van Dillen

Contrasting crocheted seams act as borders and transform five felted panels into a warm, rustic throw or accent rug.

Skill Level
■□□□

Knitted Measurements
Width (after felting, with edging) approx 50"/127cm
Length (after felting, with edging) approx 59"/150cm

Materials
- 6 3½oz/100g hanks (each approx 109yd/99m) of Noro *Kureyon Air* (wool) each in #381 Violet's Memoir (A) and #378 Turq Island (B)
- 4 hanks in #392 Mary Ellen Jasper (C) ⑥
- One pair size 13 (9mm) needles, *OR SIZE TO OBTAIN GAUGE*
- One size J/10 (6mm) crochet hook

Gauge
10 sts and 14 rows to 4"/10cm over St st using size 13 (9mm) needles, before felting.
TAKE TIME TO CHECK GAUGE.

PLACEMENT DIAGRAM

BLOCK 2		BLOCK 3
		BLOCK 4
BLOCK 1		BLOCK 5

Rug/Throw
BLOCK 1
With A, cast on 66 sts. Work in St st (k on RS, p on WS) and stripes as foll:
*6 rows A, 6 rows C; rep from * until piece measures 34½"/87cm from beg. Bind off.

BLOCK 2
With B, cast on 66 sts.
Work in St st and stripes as foll:
*6 rows B, 6 rows C; rep from * until piece measures 34½"/87cm from beg. Bind off.

BLOCK 3
With A, cast on 66 sts. Work in St st until piece measures 23"/58cm from beg. Bind off.

BLOCK 4
With B, cast on 66 sts. Work in St st and stripes as foll:
*2 rows B, 2 rows A, 2 rows C; rep from * until piece measures 23"/58cm from beg. Bind off.

BLOCK 5
With B, cast on 66 sts. Work in St st until piece measures 23"/58cm from beg. Bind off.

Finishing
Machine felt all blocks (see page 142). If necessary, block individual pieces while still wet so they will align into finished rectangle, as shown in the placement diagram. Allow pieces to fully dry before joining.

With crochet hook and C (using red sections for most contrast), arrange blocks according to placement diagram and crochet blocks tog as foll: Place blocks with RS facing up. From RS, insert hook in one piece at 3 rows or 2 sts in from edge and work 1 sc, then insert hook in corresponding st or row on opposite edge and work 1 sc, ch 3, *skip a few sts or rows and work 1 sc as before in first piece, then 1 sc in 2nd piece, ch 3; rep from * until blocks are joined.

OUTER BORDER
With crochet hook and C, and inserting hook 4 rows or 3 sts in from edge, work *1 sc, ch 3, skip a few sts or rows; rep from * around entire outside edge of blanket, working 3 sc in each corner. Fasten off. ✣

Trellis Twist

Gauge
17 sts and 24 rnds to 4"/10cm over St st using size 9 (5.5mm) needle. *TAKE TIME TO CHECK GAUGE.*

Stitch Glossary
MML3 (move marker left 3) Remove marker, sl 3 sts wyib to RH needle, pm for new beg of rnd.
MMR3 (move marker right 3) Work to 3 sts before beg of rnd marker, pm for new beg of rnd, and remove old beg of rnd marker on next rnd.
4-st RPC Sl 1 st to cn and hold to *back*, k3, p1 from cn.
4-st LPC Sl 3 sts to cn and hold to *front*, p1, k3 from cn.
6-st RC Sl 3 sts to cn and hold to *back*, k3, k3 from cn.
6-st LC Sl 3 sts to cn and hold to *front*, k3, k3 from cn.

Cowl
Cast on 120 sts. Join, taking care not to twist sts, and pm to mark beg of rnd.
Rnd 1 *P1, k2; rep from * around.
Rnd 2 Purl.
Rnds 3–5 Rep rnds 1 and 2 once more, then rep rnd 1 once more.
Rnds 6–12 Knit.

BEGIN CHART
Rnd 1 Work 12-st rep of chart 10 times around. Cont to work in this manner through rnd 46.
Rnd 47 Knit.
Rnd 48 Purl.
Rnds 49–52 Rep rnds 47 and 48 twice more.
Bind off purlwise.

Finishing
Weave in ends.
Block to measurements. ✤

Trellis Twist

Designed by Mari Tobita

Twirling cables untwist themselves into a wide lattice pattern, all set against a hazy striped background.

Skill Level
■■■□

Knitted Measurements
Circumference (bottom edge) approx 29"/73.5cm
Circumference (narrowest point) 21"/53.5cm
Length 10¼"/26cm

Materials
- 3 1¾oz/50g skeins (each approx 110yd/100m) of Noro *Kureyon* (wool) in #343 Natural/Brown/Pink/Green (4)
- One size 9 (5.5mm) circular needle, 24"/60cm long, *OR SIZE TO OBTAIN GAUGE*
- Stitch marker
- Cable needle (cn)

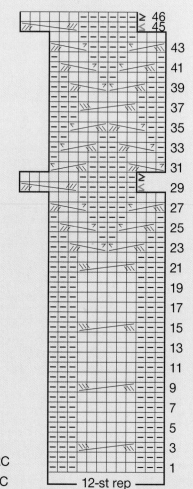

STITCH KEY
□ k	◤◥ 4-st RPC
⊟ p	◣◢ 4-st LPC
◹ MML3	◤◥◥ 6-st RC
◿ MMR3	◣◣◢ 6-st LC

12-st rep

Entre-lace Pullover

Entre-lace Pullover

Designed by Judy Hackett

Strips of geometric entrelac and linear lace provide contrast to a wide-necked pullover with an oversized fit and dolman sleeves.

Skill Level
■■■■

Size
One size fits most

Knitted Measurements
Width (lower edge above ribbing) approx 48"/122cm
Length 24"/61cm

Materials
- 14 1¾oz/50g skeins (each approx 110yd/100m) of Noro *Kureyon* (wool) in #327 Violet/Blue/Turquoise/Brown (4)
- One each sizes 8 and 9 (5 and 5.5mm) circular needle, each 40"/100cm long, *OR SIZE TO OBTAIN GAUGE*

Gauge
14 sts and 20 rows to 4"/10cm over St st using larger needle.
TAKE TIME TO CHECK GAUGE.

Notes
Circular needle is used on main body to accommodate large number of stitches. Do *not* join.

Back
With larger needle, cast on 80 sts.
Row 1 (RS) *K1, p1; rep from * to end.
Rep last row for k1, p1 rib until piece measures 2"/5cm from beg, end with a WS row.
Work in entrelac pat as foll:

BASE TRIANGLES
Row 1 (RS) K2, turn.
Row 2 P2, turn.
Row 3 K3, turn.
Row 4 P3, turn.
Row 5 K4, turn.
Row 6 P4, turn.
Row 7 K5, turn.
Row 8 P5, turn.
Row 9 K6, turn.
Row 10 P6, turn.
Row 11 K7, turn.
Row 12 P7, turn.
Row 13 K8, turn.
Row 14 P8, turn.
Row 15 K9, turn.
Row 16 P9, turn.
Row 17 K10, do *not* turn. One triangle is made. Leave these sts on hold.
Rep rows 1–17 until all 80 sts have been worked from the LH needle. There are eight 10-st triangles.

FIRST STRIP—WS RECTANGLES
LH-Edge WS Rectangle (Stockinette)
Cast on 10 sts.
Row 1 (WS) P9, p2tog using last cast-on st and first st of previous triangle (or rectangle), turn.
Row 2 (RS) K10, turn.
Rep rows 1 and 2 until all 10 sts from adjoining triangle have been worked, end with row 1. Do *not* turn.

WS Rectangle (Stockinette)
Pick-up row (WS) With RH needle, pick up and p 10 sts along edge of next triangle (or rectangle), turn.
Row 1 (RS) K10, turn.

Row 2 (WS) P9, p2tog using last st of this rectangle and first st of previous triangle (or rectangle), turn.

Rep rows 1 and 2 until all 10 sts from adjoining triangle (or rectangle) have been worked, end with row 2. Do *not* turn.

WS Rectangle (Lace)

Pick-up row (WS) With RH needle, pick up and p 10 sts along edge of next triangle (or rectangle), turn.

Row 1 (RS) K1, [yo, k2tog] 4 times, k1, turn.

Row 2 P9, p2tog using last st of this rectangle and first st of previous triangle (or rectangle), turn.

Rep rows 1 and 2 until all 10 sts from adjoining triangle (or rectangle) have been worked, end with row 2. Do *not* turn.

Cont to work 3 WS Rectangle (Stockinette), 1 WS Rectangle (Lace), and 1 WS Rectangle (Stockinette) as before (see diagram on page 82 for placement).

RH-Edge WS Rectangle (Stockinette)

Pick up row (WS) With RH needle, pick up and p 10 sts along edge of last triangle (or rectangle), turn.

Row 1 (RS) K10, turn.

Row 2 (WS) P10, turn.

Rep last 2 rows 9 times more (total of 20 rows), end with row 2, turn. There are 9 rectangles in total.

2ND STRIP—RS RECTANGLES

RH-Edge RS Rectangle (Stockinette)

Cast on 10 sts.

Row 1 (RS) K9, ssk using last st of this rectangle and first st of previous rectangle (or triangle), turn.

Row 2 (WS) P10.

Rep rows 1 and 2 until all 10 sts from adjoining rectangle have been worked, end with row 1. Do *not* turn.

RS Rectangle (Stockinette)

Pick-up row (RS) With RH needle, pick up and k 10 sts along edge of next rectangle, turn.

Row 1 (WS) P10, turn.

Row 2 (RS) K9, ssk using last st of this rectangle and first st of previous rectangle (or triangle), turn.

Rep rows 1 and 2 until all 10 sts from adjoining rectangle have been worked, end with row 2. Do *not* turn.

Cont to work 7 more RS Rectangle (Stockinette) as before.

LH-Edge RS Rectangle (Stockinette)

Pick-up row (RS) With RH needle, pick up and k 10 sts along edge of last rectangle, turn.

Row 1 (WS) P10, turn.

Row 2 (RS) K10.

Rep last 2 rows 9 times more (total of 20 rows), end with row 2, turn. There are 10 rectangles in total.

3RD STRIP—WS RECTANGLES

Work same as first strip, working in St st or lace as shown on diagram. There are 11 rectangles in total.

4TH STRIP—RS RECTANGLES

Work same as 2nd strip, working in St st or lace as shown on diagram. There are 12 squares in total.

Cont in this way, alternating RS and WS strips, adding one more rectangle on every strip and foll diagram for placement of St st and lace pats until 9 strips in total have been worked. There are 17 rectangles at end of 9th strip.

10TH STRIP—RS RECTANGLES & EDGE TRIANGLES

RH-Edge RS Triangle (Stockinette)

Row 1 (RS) Kfb, ssk, turn.

Row 2 (WS) P3, turn.

Row 3 Kfb, k1, ssk, turn.

Row 4 P4, turn.

Row 5 Kfb, k2, ssk, turn.

Row 6 P5, turn.

Row 7 Kfb, k3, ssk, turn.

Row 8 P6, turn.

Row 9 Kfb, k4, ssk, turn.

Row 10 P7, turn.

Row 11 Kfb, k5, ssk, turn.

Row 12 P8, turn.

Row 13 Kfb, k6, ssk, turn.

Row 14 P9, turn.

Row 15 Kfb, k7, ssk. Do *not* turn at end of last row. There are 10 sts on RH needle.

Cont to work 16 RS Rectangles (Stockinette) as before.

LH-Edge RS Triangle (Stockinette)

Pick-up row (RS) With RH needle, pick up and k 10 sts along edge of last rectangle, turn.

Next row (WS) P10, turn.

Row 1 Sl 1, k9, turn.

Row 2 P2tog, p8, turn.

Row 3 Sl 1, k8, turn.

Row 4 P2tog, p7, turn.

Row 5 Sl 1, k7, turn.

Row 6 P2tog, p6, turn.

Row 7 Sl 1, k6, turn.

Row 8 P2tog, p5, turn.

Row 9 Sl 1, k5, turn.
Row 10 P2tog, p4, turn.
Row 11 Sl 1, k4, turn.
Row 12 P2tog, p3, turn.
Row 13 Sl 1, k3, turn.
Row 14 P2tog, p2, turn.
Row 15 Sl 1, k2, turn.
Row 16 P2tog, p1, turn.
Row 17 Sl 1, k1, turn.
Row 18 P2tog—1 st rem on LH needle, turn.
There are 16 rectangles in total and one edge triangle at each end.

11TH STRIP—BOUND-OFF WS RECTANGLES
WS Bound-Off Rectangle (Lace)
Pick-up row (WS) With RH needle, pick up and p 9 sts along edge of triangle—10 sts on RH needle, turn.
Row 1 (RS) K1, [yo, k2tog] 4 times, k1, turn.
Row 2 P9, p2tog using last st of this rectangle and first st of previous rectangle, turn.
Rep rows 1 and 2 until 9 sts from adjoining rectangle have been worked, end with a RS row, turn.
Last row (WS) Bind off sts of this rectangle purlwise, working last p2tog before binding off last st. Cut yarn and fasten off last st.

Next 5 Rectangles
Rejoin yarn and work same as WS Bound-Off Rectangle (Lace), but pick up and p 10 sts along edge of next rectangle and foll diagram for placement of St st and lace pats.

Next 4 Rectangles
Work same as WS rectangles on first strip, foll diagram for placement of St st and lace pats.

Last 7 Rectangles
Work same as WS Bound-Off Rectangle (Lace), but pick up and p 10 sts along edge of next rectangle and foll diagram for placement of St st and lace pats.
There are 17 rectangles in total.

12TH STRIP—RS TOP TRIANGLES
RS Top Triangle
Pick-up row (RS) With RH needle, pick up and k 10 sts along edge of rectangle before first rectangle with live stitches that were not bound off, then k first stitch on LH needle—11 sts, turn.
Row 1 (WS) P2tog, p7, p2tog, turn.
Row 2 (RS) K10, turn.
Row 3 P2tog, p6, p2tog, turn.
Row 4 K9, turn.
Row 5 P2tog, p5, p2tog, turn.

Row 6 K8, turn.
Row 7 P2tog, p4, p2tog, turn.
Row 8 K7, turn.
Row 9 P2tog, p3, p2tog, turn.
Row 10 K6, turn.
Row 11 P2tog, p2, p2tog, turn.
Row 12 K5, turn.
Row 13 P2tog, p1, p2tog, turn.
Row 14 K4, turn.
Row 15 P2tog, p2tog, turn.
Row 16 K3, turn.
Row 17 P1, p2tog, turn.
Row 18 K3tog—1 st rem on RH needle.

Work 3 more RS Top Triangles as foll:
*Pick-up row (RS) With RH needle, pick up and k 9 sts along edge of next rectangle, then k first stitch on LH needle — 11 sts, turn.
Work rows 1–18 same as first RS Top Triangle. Rep from * twice more. After working fourth and final RS Top Triangle, cut yarn and fasten off last st. These 4 end triangles form the back neck.

Front
Work same as back foll diagram for placement of St st and lace pats, end with 9th strip.

10TH STRIP—EDGE RS TRIANGLES, RS RECTANGLES, & TOP RS TRIANGLES
Work RH-Edge RS Triangle (Stockinette) same as back.
Work 7 RS Rectangles (Stockinette) as before. Bind off 10 sts on the 7th rectangle.
Work 2 RS Top Triangles same as back.
Work 7 RS Rectangles (Stockinette) as before.
Work LH-Edge RS Triangle (Stockinette) same as back.

11TH STRIP—WS RECTANGLES AND NECK SHAPING
Pick-up row (WS) With RH needle, pick up and p 9 sts along edge of triangle—10 sts on RH needle, turn.
Work 7 WS Rectangles same as back, foll diagram for placement of St st and lace pats. Bind off 10 sts on 7th rectangle. Cut yarn.
Rejoin to other side of neck. Work 7 WS Rectangles same as back, foll diagram for placement of St st and lace pats. Bind off 10 sts on 7th rectangle.

12TH SHOULDER STRIP—
BOUND-OFF RS RECTANGLES & EDGE TRIANGLES
Work rows 1–14 same as RH-Edge RS Triangle (Stockinette) on 10th strip of back.
Row 15 Bind off knitwise, working last ssk before binding off last st—1 st rem on RH needle. Do *not* turn.

BACK

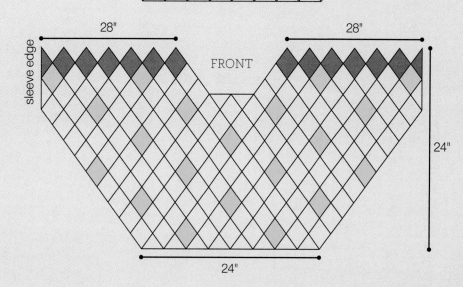

sleeve edge

◇ Lace

◇ Stockinette

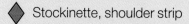◆ Stockinette, shoulder strip

28"   28"

sleeve edge

FRONT

24"

24"

24"

First 6 Rectangles

Pick–up row (RS) With RH needle, pick up and k 9 sts along edge of next rectangle—10 sts on RH needle, turn.

Work same as RS Rectangle (Stockinette), but bind off last RS row and work last ssk before binding off last st—1 st rem on RH needle. Do *not* turn. Fasten off last st on last rectangle at neck edge.

Last 6 Rectangles

Skip neck opening and rejoin yarn to next rectangle. With RH needle, pick up and k 10 sts along edge of next rectangle (for foll 5 rectangles only pick up 9 sts), and work same as first 6 RS Rectangles (Stockinette).

Work rows 1–18 of last LH-Edge RS Triangle (Stockinette) same as 10th strip of back. Fasten off last st.

Finishing

Match shoulder strip on front into spaces at top of back and sew along the seams.

CUFFS

With RS facing and smaller needle, pick up and k 40 sts evenly along one sleeve edge. Work back and forth in rows in k1, p1 rib for 2"/5cm. Bind off loosely in rib.

Work in same way along other sleeve edge.

Sew side and cuff seams.

NECKBAND

With RS facing and smaller needle, pick up and k 112 sts evenly around neck edge. Join to work in rnds and pm for beg of rnd.

Next rnd *K1, p1; rep from * around.

Rep last rnd for 1"/2.5cm. Bind off loosely in rib.

Weave in ends. Block to measurements. ✤

Tilted Lace Scarf

Tilted Lace Scarf

Designed by Susan Ashcroft

Simple increases and decreases make a gorgeous pattern on the bias, creating the illusion of pointed tips.

Skill Level
■■□□

Knitted Measurements
Length (tip to tip) 86½"/219.5cm
Width 8½"/20.5cm

Materials
■ 4 1¾oz/50g skeins (each approx 110yd/100m) of Noro *Kureyon* (wool) in #392 Mary Ellen Jasper ④
■ One pair size 10 (6mm) needles, *OR SIZE TO OBTAIN GAUGE*

Gauge
13 sts and 19 rows to 4"/10cm over bias pat using size 10 (6mm) needles.
TAKE TIME TO CHECK GAUGE.

Bias Pattern
(multiple of 7 sts plus 11)
Row 1 (RS) Kfb, *k2, yo, p1, p3tog, p1, yo; rep from * to last 10 sts, k2, yo, p1, p3tog, p1, yo, k1, k2tog.
Row 2 and all WS rows Sl 1 purlwise wyif, p to last st, sl 1 purlwise wyif.
Rows 3, 7, 11, 15, 19, 23, and 27 Kfb, k to last 2 sts, k2tog.
Row 5 Kfb, p2tog, yo, *k2, yo, p1, p3tog, p1, yo; rep from * to last 8 sts, k2, yo, p1, p2tog, p1, k2tog.
Row 9 Kfb, p1, p2tog, p1, yo; *k2, yo, p1, p3tog, p1, yo; rep from * to last 6 sts, k2, yo, p2tog, k2tog.
Row 13 Kfb, k1, yo, p1, p3tog, p1, yo, *k2, yo, p1, p3tog, p1, yo; rep from * to last 4 sts, k2, k2tog.
Row 17 Kfb, k1, *k2, yo, p1, p3tog, p1, yo; rep from * to last 9 sts, k2, yo, p1, p3tog, p1, yo, k2tog.
Row 21 Kfb, p1, p2tog, yo, *k2, yo, p1, p3tog, p1, yo; rep from * to last 7 sts, k2, yo, p1, p2tog, k2tog.
Row 25 Kfb, yo, p1, p3tog, p1, yo, *k2, yo, p1, p3tog, p1, yo; rep from * to last 5 sts, k3, k2tog.
Row 28 Rep row 2.
Rep rows 1–28 for bias pat.

Notes
1) The bias of this scarf is created by increasing at the beginning of every RS row and decreasing at the end of every RS row.
2) Bias pattern can be worked from chart or written instructions.

Scarf
Using cable cast-on method, cast on 46 sts.
Set-up row 1 (RS) Kfb, k to last 2 sts, k2tog.
Set-up row 2 (WS) Sl 1 purlwise wyif, p to last st, sl 1 purlwise wyif.
Work in bias pat until piece measures approx 86½"/219.5cm from beg, end with row 2, 6, 10, 14, 18, 22, or 26 of pat.
Bind off all sts knitwise.

Finishing
Weave in ends. Block to measurements. ✤

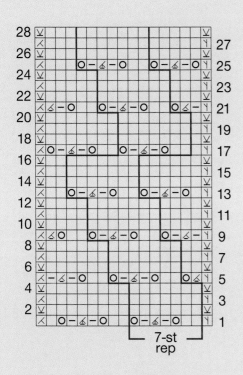

STITCH KEY

☐ k on RS, p on WS

⊟ p on RS, k on WS

☒ slip 1 purlwise wyif on WS

⅂ kfb

◎ yo

◺ k2tog

◸ p2tog

◿ p3tog

Puff Love

Puff Love

Designed by Angela Tong

Casual cool days call for a whimsical puffed hat with yarnovers that create a subtle faux-ribbing effect.

Skill Level
■ ■ □ □

Knitted Measurements
Brim circumference 21½"/54.5cm
Height 8½"/20.5cm

Materials
■ 2 1¾oz/50g skeins (each approx 110yd/100m) of Noro *Kureyon* (wool) in #188 Moss/Purples/Navy/Black/Grey (4)
■ One each sizes 6 and 8 (4 and 5mm) circular needles, 16"/40cm long, *OR SIZE TO OBTAIN GAUGE*
■ One set (5) size 8 (5mm) double-pointed needles (dpn)
■ Stitch marker

Gauge
19 sts and 24 rnds to 4"/10cm over puff st using larger needles. *TAKE TIME TO CHECK GAUGE.*

Puff Stitch
(multiple of 3 sts)
Rnd 1 *P2, yo, k1, yo; rep from * around—2 sts inc'd in each rep.
Rnds 2 and 3 *P2, k3; rep from * around.
Rnd 4 *P2, k3tog; rep from * around—2 sts dec'd in each rep.
Rnds 5–8 Knit.
Rep rnds 1–8 for puff st.

Hat
With smaller circular needle, cast on 92 sts. Join to work in rnds, taking care not to twist sts on needle, and pm to mark beg of rnd.
Rnd 1 *K2, p2; rep from * around.
Rep rnd 1 for k2, p2 rib until piece measures 2"/5cm from beg.
Inc rnd K2, *kfb, k8; rep from * around—102 sts.
Change to larger circular needle. Knit 2 rnds.

BEGIN PUFF STITCH
Work rnds 1–8 of puff st 3 times, then work rnds 1–4 once more.

CROWN SHAPING
Note Change to dpn, dividing sts evenly over 4 needles, when there are too few sts to fit comfortably on circular needle.
Rnd 1 [K2tog, k49] twice—100 sts.
Rnd 2 *K3, k2tog; rep from * around—80 sts.
Rnd 3 Knit.
Rnd 4 *K2, k2tog; rep from * around—60 sts.
Rnd 5 Knit.
Rnd 6 *K2tog; rep from * around—30 sts.
Rnd 7 Knit.
Rnd 8 *K2tog; rep from * around—15 sts.
Rnd 9 Knit.
Rnd 10 K1, [k2tog] 7 times—8 sts.
Rnd 11 [K2tog] 4 times—4 sts.
Cut yarn, leaving a long end. Pull tail through sts on needles and draw up tightly to close.

Finishing
Weave in ends. Block to measurements. ❖

Color Waves

Color Waves

Designed by Alexandra Davidoff

Arranging fourteen textured strips of seven unique colorways, with tasseled pompoms anchoring each end, offers nearly limitless color possibilities.

Skill Level
■■□□

Knitted Measurements
Width 55"/139.5cm
Length (excluding pompoms and tassels) 53¼"/135.5cm

Materials
- 4 1¾oz/50g skeins (each approx 110yd/100m) of Noro *Kureyon* (wool) each in #389 River Birch (A), #392 Mary Ellen Jasper (B), #378 Turq Island (C), #381 Violet's Memoir (D), #263 Tomato/Black/Browns (E), #332 Lime/Olive/Jade/Purple (F), and #40 Aqua/Purple Multi (G) (■4■)
- One pair size 10 (6mm) needles, *OR SIZE TO OBTAIN GAUGE*
- Removable stitch marker
- One small pompom maker
- Cardboard strip, 5"/12.5cm wide for tassels

Gauge
15½ sts and 22½ rows to 4"/10cm over ribbed box pat st using size 10 (6mm) needles.
TAKE TIME TO CHECK GAUGE.

Ribbed Box Pattern Stitch
(17 sts)
Row 1 (RS) Sl 1 wyif, k7, [p1, k1] 4 times, k1.
Row 2 Sl 1 wyif, [p1, k1] 4 times, k8.
Rows 3–12 Rep rows 1 and 2 five times more.
Row 13 Sl 1 wyif, [k1, p1] 4 times, k8.
Row 14 Sl 1 wyif, k7, [k1, p1] 4 times, k1.
Rows 15–24 Rep rows 13 and 14 five times more.
Rep rows 1–24 for ribbed box pat st.

Notes
1) Strips are nearly identical on both sides, with only a slight difference. Mark the right side of the work.
2) Each strip measures approximately 4½"/11.5cm wide before seaming.
3) Ribbed box pattern stitch can be worked from chart or written instructions.

Blanket
STRIP 1
With A, cast on 17 sts. Work in ribbed box pat st until piece measures 53"/134.5cm, end with row 12. Bind off all sts knitwise or in rib as they appear.

STRIPS 2–14
Work 1 more strip with A, then 2 strips each with rem colors.

Finishing
Weave in ends. Using mattress st, sew strips tog foll assembly diagram, or in desired order. Block to measurements.

POMPOMS AND TASSELS
Make 4 tassels with each color, leaving 12"/30.5cm long tails at top of each tassel.
Make 4 pompoms with each color, using long tails from tassels to secure each pompom above tassel.
Sew a pompom/tassel to each end of strips of corresponding colors, using rem long tails to attach to blanket. ❖

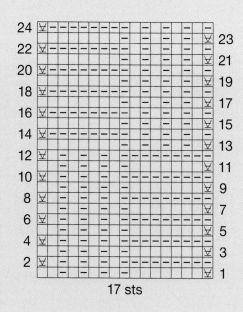

17 sts

STITCH KEY

☐ k on RS, p on WS

− p on RS, k on WS

☒ slip 1 wyif

ASSEMBLY DIAGRAM

E B D C G F A A F G C D B E

Seedling

Seedling

Designed by Rosemary Drysdale

Working in seed stitch with two balls of the same self-striping colorway to stagger the color sequence makes for a simple, multi-seasonal scarf.

Skill Level
■□□□

Knitted Measurements
Length 86"/218.5cm
Width 10½"/26.5cm

Materials
■ 6 1¾oz/50g skeins (each approx 110yd/100m) of Noro *Kureyon* (wool) in #102 Pinks/Orange/Purple/Blue ④
■ One pair size 10 (6mm) needles, *OR SIZE TO OBTAIN GAUGE*

Gauge
14 sts and 25 rows to 4"/10cm over seed st using size 10 (6mm) needles.
TAKE TIME TO CHECK GAUGE.

Seed Stitch
(odd number of sts)
Row 1 (RS) K1, *p1, k1; rep from * to end.
Rep row 1 for seed st.

Note
Label 3 skeins as A and 3 skeins as B.

Scarf
With A, cast on 37 sts.
Rows 1 and 2 With A, work 2 rows in seed st.
Rows 3 and 4 With B, work 2 rows in seed st.
Rep rows 1–4 until scarf is approx 86"/218.5cm in length, end with row 2 or 4. Bind off in pat color used for last row.

Finishing
Weave in ends. Block to measurements. ✣

Wicker Lace Pullover

Wicker Lace Pullover

Designed by Yoko Hatta

An oversized, drop-shoulder pullover is reminiscent of wicker as neutral tones play across alternating strips of stockinette and simple lace.

Skill Level
■ ■ ▢ ▢

Sizes
Instructions are written for sizes Small (Medium, Large, X-Large). Shown in size Small.

Knitted Measurements
Bust 57 (60, 62½, 65)"/144.5 (152, 158.5, 165)cm
Length (back) 27"/68.5cm
Length (front) 25"/63.5cm
Upper arm 13 (14, 15, 16)"/33 (35.5, 38, 40.5)cm

Materials
■ 4 (5, 5, 5) 1¾oz/50g skeins (each approx 110yd/100m) of Noro *Kureyon* (wool) each in #149 Brown/Grey/Taupe (A) and #211 Naturals (B) (❹)
■ One size 9 (5.5mm) circular needle, 24"/60cm long, *OR SIZE TO OBTAIN GAUGE*
■ One spare size 9 (5.5mm) needle
■ Stitch holders
■ Stitch marker

Gauge
12 sts and 21 rows to 4"/10cm over eyelet stripe pat using size 9 (5.5mm) needle.
TAKE TIME TO CHECK GAUGE.

Eyelet Stripe Pattern
(over an even number of sts)
Row 1 (RS) With B, k1, *k2tog, yo; rep from * to last st, k1.
Row 2 With B, purl.
Row 3 With B, k1, *yo, SKP; rep from * to last st, k1.
Row 4 With B, purl.
Row 5 With A, knit.
Row 6 With A, purl.
Rows 7 and 8 Rep rows 5 and 6.
Rep rows 1–8 for eyelet stripe pat.

Notes
1) Circular needle is used to accommodate large number of stitches. Do *not* join.
2) Back is longer than front.

Back
With circular needle and A, cast on 88 (92, 96, 100) sts. Knit 4 rows. Work in eyelet stripe pat until piece measures approx 26¼"/66.5cm from beg, end with pat row 4 in color B.

NECK SHAPING
Next row (RS) With A, k26 (28, 30, 32), k2tog, k1, sl next 30 sts to st holder; join 2nd ball of A, k1, SKP, k to end.
Using separate balls of yarn, work both sides at once, as foll:
Next row (WS) Purl across each side.
Next row *First Side*: K to last 3 sts, k2tog, k1; *Second Side*: K1, SKP, k to end.
Next row Purl across each side.
Place sts each side on separate st holders.

Front
Work same as back until piece measures approx 24¼"/61.5cm from beg, end with pat row 4 in color B.

NECK SHAPING
Work same as for back.

Sleeves (make 2)
With circular needle and A, cast on 40 (42, 46, 48) sts. Knit 4 rows. Work in eyelet stripe pat until piece measures 10½"/26.5cm from beg. Bind off.

Finishing

Place shoulder sts on needles. With RS held tog, join shoulders using 3-needle bind-off (see page 142).

With RS facing and circular needle, k30 from back neck holder, pick up and k 6 sts along neck shaping, k30 from front neck holder, and pick up and k 6 sts along neck shaping—72 sts. Join to work in rnds and pm to mark beg of rnd. Purl 1 rnd, k 1 rnd, bind off loosely purlwise.

Place marker 6½ (7, 7½, 8)"/16.5 (18, 19, 20.5)cm down from shoulder seam on front and back. Sew sleeves to armholes between markers. Sew underarm seams.

Sew side seams, leaving bottom 4"/10cm on front and bottom 6"/15cm on back unseamed. Reinforce join at top of flaps with extra sts.

Block finished piece lightly. ❧

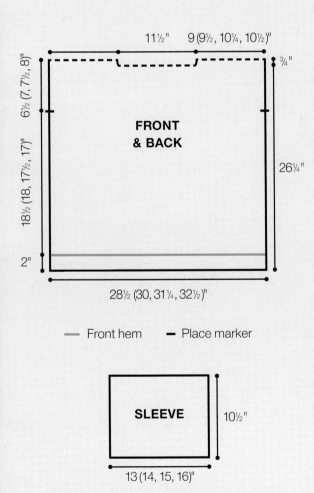

103

Color Punch Scarf

Color Punch Scarf

Designed by Anne Jones

Punchy waves of color undulate through a unique feather-and-fan slip-stitch pattern.

Skill Level
■■□□

Knitted Measurements
Width approx 14½"/37cm
Length approx 62"/157.5cm

Materials
- 7 1¾oz/50g skeins (each approx 110yd/100m) of Noro *Kureyon* (wool) in #374 Hot Pink/Cocoa/Lime 〔4〕
- One pair size 8 (5mm) needles, *OR SIZE TO OBTAIN GAUGE*

Gauge
21 sts and 26 rows to 4"/10cm over color punch pat using size 8 (5mm) needles.
TAKE TIME TO CHECK GAUGE.

Note
Color punch pattern can be worked from charts 1 and 2 or written instructions.

Color Punch Pattern
Rows 1, 3, and 5 (RS) K2, p1, *sl 2 wyif, p1; rep from * to last 2 sts, k2.
Rows 2, 4, and 6 K2, p to last 2 sts, k2.
Row 7 K3, *k1, yo, k5, ssk, p1, [k1, p1] 3 times, k2tog, k5, yo; rep from * to last 5 sts, k5.
Row 8 K2, p3 *p1, yo, p5, p2tog, k1, [p1, k1] twice, p2tog tbl, p5, yo, p2; rep from * to last 3 sts, p1, k2.
Row 9 K3, *k3, yo, k5, ssk, p1, k1, p1, k2tog, k5, yo, k2; rep from * to last 5 sts, k5.
Row 10 K2, p3, *p3, yo, p5, p2tog, k1, p2tog tbl, p5, yo, p4; rep from * to last 3 sts, p1, k2.
Row 11 K3, *k5, yo, k5, sssk, k5, yo, k4; rep from * to last 5 sts, k5.
Row 12 K2, p to last 2 sts, k2.
Rep rows 1–12 for color punch pat.

Scarf
Cast on 74 sts.
Work color punch pattern 33 times and then work rows 1–5 once more, or work chart 1 and then chart 2 thirty-three times and then work rows 1–5 of chart 1 once more.
Bind off purlwise on WS.

Finishing
Weave in ends. Block to measurements. ❖

CHART 1

6 | 4 | 2 | 5 | 3 | 1
3-st rep

STITCH KEY

□ k on RS, p on WS

– p on RS, k on WS

⊻ slip 1 purlwise wyif on RS

○ yo

⊠ ssk on RS, p2tog tbl on WS

⊠ k2tog on RS, p2tog on WS

⊠ sssk

CHART 2

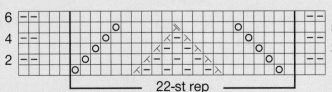

6 | 4 | 2 | 5 | 3 | 1
22-st rep

Fair and Square

Fair and Square

Designed by Valentina Devine

This cardigan won't easily be forgotten with its clever construction and kaleidoscopic spin on a chessboard.

Skill Level
■■■■

Sizes
Instructions are written for sizes Small (Medium, Large, X-Large). Shown in size Medium.

Knitted Measurements
Bust (closed) 38 (42, 44, 47½)"/96.5 (106.5, 111.5, 120.5)cm
Length 20 (20, 23, 23)"/51 (51, 58.5, 58.5)cm
Upperarm 16 (16, 18, 18)"/40.5 (40.5, 45.5, 45.5)cm

Materials
■ 6 (6, 7, 7) 1¾oz/50g skeins (each approx 110yd/100m) of Noro *Kureyon* (wool) each in #40 Aqua/Purple Multi (A) and #359 Blues/Lilac/Yellow (B) (**4**)
■ One size 10 (6mm) circular needle, 24"/60cm long,
OR SIZE TO OBTAIN GAUGE

■ One extra size 10 (6mm) needle for 3-needle bind-off
■ One pair size 8 (5mm) needles
■ Stitch markers
■ Stitch holders
■ Five ½"/13mm buttons

Gauge
17 sts and 18 rows to 4"/10cm over checkerboard pat using size 10 (6mm) needle.
TAKE TIME TO CHECK GAUGE.

Notes
1) When changing colors in block pat, twist yarns on WS to prevent holes in work. To avoid long floats, twist yarns every 2 or 3 sts.
2) The body is worked in one piece to the underarm.
Back, left front, and right front are worked separately to the shoulder. Sleeve sts are cast on and worked along with the body pieces.

Corrugated Rib
(multiple of 4 sts)
Row 1 (RS) *With A, k2; with B p2, rep from * to end.
Row 2 *With B, k2; with A, p2, rep from * to end.
Rep rows 1 and 2 for corrugated rib.

Checkerboard Pattern
(multiple of 8 sts)
Rows 1 and 3 (RS) *With A, k4; with B, k4, rep from * to end.
Rows 2 and 4 (WS) *With B, p4; with A, p4, rep from * to end.
Rows 5 and 7 *With B, k4; with A, k4, rep from * to end.
Rows 6 and 8 *With A, p4; with B, p4; rep from * to end.
Rep rows 1–8 for checkerboard pat.

Body
With circular needle and A, cast on 160 (176, 184, 200) sts. Work in corrugated rib for 5¾ (5¾, 6, 6)"/14.5 (14.5, 15.5, 15.5)cm.
Work in checkerboard pat until rows 1–8 have been worked 3 (3, 4, 4) times, then work rows 1–4 once more—piece measures approx 12 (12, 14, 14)"/30.5 (30.5, 35.5, 35.5)cm from beg. Cut yarn.

DIVIDE FOR BACK AND FRONTS
Sl first 40 (44, 46, 50) sts to a st holder for right front, sl last 40 (44, 46, 50) sts to a st holder for left front.

Back

Join yarn to rem 80 (88, 92, 100) sts on needle to work a RS row. Beg with a pat row 5, cont in checkerboard pat as foll:

Next row (RS) Cast on 48 (48, 50, 56) sts onto LH needle using cable cast-on, beg with 4B (4A, 4A, 2B), cont in checkerboard pat to end.

Next row (WS) Cast on 48 (48, 50, 56) sts onto LH needle using cable cast-on, beg with 4A (4B, 4B, 2A), cont in checkerboard pat to end—176 (184, 192, 212) sts.

Work even in pat for 30 (30, 34, 34) rows more.

SHAPE NECK

Next row (RS) Work 76 (80, 84, 94) sts, join 2nd ball of yarn and bind off center 24 sts, work to end. Working both sides at once, work even for 3 rows more. Sl sts each side onto separate holder—sleeve measures approx 8 (8, 9, 9)"/20.5 (20.5, 23, 23)cm. Cut yarn.

Left Front

Sl left front sts from st holder to needle to work next row from RS. Beg with a pat row 5, cont in checkerboard pat as foll:

Next row (RS) Cast on 48 (48, 50, 56) sts onto LH needle using cable cast-on for sleeve, beg with 4B (4A, 4B, 2A) work cast-on sts, then cont in pat on left front sts—88 (92, 96, 106) sts.

Work 1 row even in pats as established.

SHAPE NECK

Cont in checkerboard pat, work as foll:

Dec row (RS) Work to last 3 sts, k2tog, k1.

Rep dec row every other row 11 times more—76 (80, 84, 94) sts. Work even until same amount of rows have been worked as left back. Place sts on a st holder.

Right Front

Sl right front sts from st holder to needle to work next row from RS.

Next row (RS) Cont in pat, work row 5 of checkerboard pat.

Next row (WS) Cast on 48 (48, 50, 56) sts onto LH needle using cable cast-on for sleeve, beg with 4A (4B, 4A, 2B), work pat row 6—88 (92, 96, 106) sts.

SHAPE NECK

Cont in checkerboard pat, work as foll:

Dec row (RS) K1, k2tog, work to end.

Rep dec row every other row 11 times more—76 (80, 84, 94) sts. Work even until same amount of rows have been worked as right back. Leave sts on needle.

Finishing

Slip sts from right back holder to extra size 10 (6mm) needle, ready to work WS row. With RS held together, join right shoulder/sleeve sts tog using 3-needle bind-off (see page 142). Join left shoulder/sleeve sts in same way.

SLEEVE CUFF

With RS facing, size 8 (5mm) needles and A, pick up and k 36 (36, 40, 40) sts evenly along cuff edge of sleeve. Work in corrugated rib for 5"/13cm. Bind off.
Rep for other sleeve edge.
Sew sleeve and cuff seams.

BUTTON BAND

With RS facing, size 10 (6mm) circular needle and A, pick up and k sts evenly around right front, back neck, and left front, making sure number of sts are same for right and left fronts. Place markers on left front for 5 buttons, the first one ½"/1.5cm from cast-on edge and the other 4 spaced 3"/7.5cm apart.

Next row (WS) With A, p2; *with B, p2; with A, p2, rep from * to end. Cont in St st (k on RS, p on RS) in colors as established as foll:

Buttonhole row (RS) With A, k2; bind off 2 sts (opposite first marker), [work to opposite next marker, bind off 2 sts] 4 times, work to end.

Purl next row, matching colors and cast on 2 sts over each set of bound-off sts.

Bind off all sts knitwise.

Sew on buttons.

Weave in ends. Block to measurements. ❖

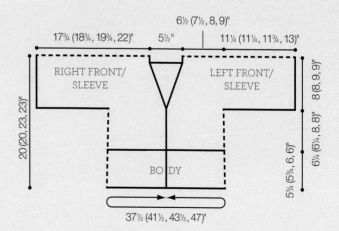

Chain Link Shawlette

Chain Link Shawlette

Designed by Cheryl Murray

Ends of I-cords are joined to create a unique lower hem of a graphic, shoulder-grazing shawl.

Skill Level
■■■□

Knitted Measurements
Width approx 70"/178cm
Length 13½"/34.5cm

Materials
■ 6 1¾oz/50g skeins (each approx 110yd/100m) of Noro *Kureyon* (wool) in #381 Violet's Memoir (4)
■ One each sizes 9 and 10 (5.5 and 6mm) circular needles, 32"/80cm long, *OR SIZE TO OBTAIN GAUGE*
■ One pair size 9 (5.5mm) double-pointed needles (dpn)
■ Stitch markers

Gauge
16 sts and 31 rows to 4"/10cm over garter st using larger needles. *TAKE TIME TO CHECK GAUGE.*

Short Row Wrap & Turn (w&t)
On RS row (on WS row)
1) Wyib (wyif), sl next st purlwise.
2) Move yarn between the needles to the front (back).
3) Sl the same st back to LH needle. Turn work. One st is wrapped.
4) When working the wrapped st, insert RH needle under the wrap and work it tog with corresponding st on needle.

Note
Circular needle is used to accommodate large number of stitches. Do *not* join.

Shawlette
LOOP EDGING
With 2 dpn, cast on 3 sts. Work I-cord as foll: *Knit one row. Without turning work, slide the sts back to the opposite end of needle to work next row from RS. Pull yarn tightly from the end of the row. Rep from * until I-cord measures 4"/10cm long. Sl sts for each I-cord to smaller circular needle.
Make 43 more I-cords in same way, slipping sts to smaller circular needle.

Joining row (RS) Knit across 6 sts of first two I-cords, bring cast-on edge of first I-cord behind 2nd I-cord, pick up and k 3 sts from cast-on edge, *knit 3 sts from next I-cord, bring cast-on end of previous I-cord behind sts just worked, pick up and k 3 sts from cast-on edge; rep from * until cast-on edge of final I-cord rem, pick up and k 3 sts from cast-on edge of final I-cord—264 sts.
Knit 3 rows.
Eyelet row (RS) K2tog, *yo, k2tog; rep from * to end of row—263 sts.
Knit 1 row.
Change to larger circular needle.

BEGIN SHORT ROWS
Short row 1 K149, pm, w&t.
Short row 2 K35, pm, w&t.
Short row 3 K to marker, remove marker, k4, pm, w&t.
Rep short row 3 twenty-five times more—139 sts between markers.
Short row 4 K to marker, remove marker, k2, pm, w&t.
Rep short row 4 until all sts are worked.
Bind off loosely.

Finishing
Weave in ends. Block to measurements. ✿

Brick Lane

Brick Lane

Designed by Wei Wilkins

Embraced on each end by brick wall panels, center chevron stripes increase this shawl's angular aspect.

Skill Level
■ ■ ■ ■

Knitted Measurements
Length 70"/177.5cm
Width 23"/58.5cm

Materials
- 8 1¾oz/50g skeins (each approx 110yd/100m) of Noro *Kureyon* (wool) in #211 Naturals (MC) (4)
- 2 skeins each in #149 Brown/Grey/Taupe (A) and #263 Tomato/Black/Browns (B)
- Two size 9 (5.5mm) circular needles, each 36"/90cm long, *OR SIZE TO OBTAIN GAUGE*
- One size 8 (5mm) circular needle, 47"/120cm long
- Stitch markers
- Small safety pin

Gauge
15 sts and 23 rows to 4"/10cm over brick pat using larger needle.
TAKE TIME TO CHECK GAUGE.

Stitch Glossary
DWS (double-wrapped stitch) Knit stitch, wrapping yarn twice *very loosely* around needle.
MES (make elongated stitch) With RH needle, reach behind work and knit into purl bump of MC stitch below DWS for a M1, then slip DWS purlwise, allowing extra wrap to drop off needle, to create the elongated stitch (ES). Carry this elongated stitch, slipping it and keeping it to RS of work as you work the next 5 rows.

Brick Pattern
(multiple of 10 sts plus 3)
Row 1 (WS) With A, k10, *DWS, k9; rep from * to last 3 sts, DWS, k2.
Row 2 With MC, k2, MES, *k9, MES; rep from * to last 10 sts, k10.
Rows 3, 5, and 7 With MC, purl (sl all ES, keeping them at RS of work).
Rows 4 and 6 With MC, knit (sl all ES, keeping them at RS of work).
Row 8 With A, k2, k ES tog with the M1 st, *k9, k ES tog with the M1 st; rep from * to last 10 sts, k10.
Row 9 With A, k5, DWS, *k9, DWS; rep from * to last 7 sts, k7.
Row 10 With MC, k7, MES, *k9, MES; rep from * to last 5 sts, k5.
Rows 11, 13, and 15 With MC, purl (sl all ES, keeping them at RS of work).
Rows 12 and 14 With MC, knit (sl all ES, keeping them at RS of work).
Row 16 With A, k7, k ES tog with the M1 st, *k9, k ES tog with the M1 st; rep from * to last 5 sts, k5.
Rep rows 1–16 for brick pat.

Note
Circular needles are used to accommodate large number of stitches. Do *not* join.

Center Chevron
With larger needle and MC, cast on 3 sts. Purl 1 row.
Row 1 (RS) K1, M1, (k1, yo, k1) into center st, M1, k1—7 sts.
Rows 2 and 4 Purl.
Row 3 K1, M1, k2, M1, pm, k1, M1, k2, M1, k1—11 sts.
Row 5 Join B, k1, M1, k to marker, M1, sm, k1, M1, k to last st, M1, k1—4 sts inc'd.
Row 6 With B, knit. Cut B.
Rows 7 and 9 With MC, k1, M1, k to marker, M1, sm, k1, M1, k to last st, M1, k1—4 sts inc'd.
Rows 8 and 10 Purl.
Rep rows 5–10 seventeen times more—227 sts.
With RS facing, place last 113 sts on 2nd circular needle, then place center st on safety pin.

First Half
Work one half of shawl over first 113 sts on first needle, as foll:
Note Inc at beg of RS row is offset by dec at end of RS row. St count rem same until corner shaping.

Next row (RS) With MC, k1, M1, k to last 3 sts, ssk, k1.
Next row With MC, purl.
Next row With A, k1, M1, k to last 3 sts, ssk, k1.

BEGIN BRICK PATTERN
Cont in brick pat, inc at beg and dec at end of every RS row, as foll:
Row 1 (WS) With A, k10, *DWS, k9; rep from * to last 3 sts, DWS, k2.
Row 2 (RS) With MC, k1, M1, k1, *MES, k9; rep from * to last 3 sts, ssk, k1.
Rows 3, 5, and 7 With MC, purl, (sl all ES, keeping them at RS of work).
Rows 4 and 6 With MC, k1, M1, k to last 3 sts (sl all ES, keeping them at RS of work), ssk, k1.
Row 8 (RS) With A, k1, M1, k4, *k ES tog with the M1 st, k9; rep from * to last 3 sts, ssk, k1.
Cont in this way, work k1, M1 at beg and ssk, k1 at end of every RS row, work every WS row even for diagonal pat, and work brick pat as established. Only incorporate new DWS when enough sts are available (at least 6 sts to accommodate decreases at edge, do not work DWS into first or last st of WS row).
When there are a total of 6 brick blocks, end with pat row 1 or 9.
Piece measures approx 7"/18cm from beg of brick pat.

SHAPE CORNER
Cont in pat, work as foll:
Dec row (RS) K1, k2tog, work in pat to last 3 sts, ssk, k1.
Cont in brick pat, dec 1 st at each end of every RS row until 5 sts rem. Only incorporate new DWS when enough sts are available (at least 6 sts to accommodate decreases at edges, do not work DWS into first or last st of row).
Next row (RS) K1, S2KP, k1, then sl the 3 sts to LH needle and S2KP, fasten off last st.

Second Half
Work rem half of shawl over last 113 sts on 2nd circular needle, as foll:
Note Inc and dec are reversed for 2nd half. Dec at beg of RS row is offset by inc at end of RS row. St count rem same until corner shaping.
Next row (RS) With MC, k2tog, k to last st, M1, k1.
Next row With MC, purl.
Next row With A, k2tog, k to last st, M1, k1.

BEGIN DIAGONAL BRICK PATTERN
Row 1 (WS) With A, k2, *DWS, k9; rep from * to last st, k1.
Work same as for first half, with reversed dec/inc shaping, as described in note above. Only incorporate new DWS when enough sts are available (at least 6 sts to accommodate decreases at edge, do not work DWS into first or last st of WS row).
When there are a total of 6 brick blocks, end with 2 pat rows in A.
Piece measures approx 7"/18cm from beg of diagonal brick pat.

Work shape corner same as for first half.

BORDERS
With B and smaller needle, pick up and k 3 sts for every 4 rows (including st from safety pin) around all 4 edges. Join to work in rnds and pm to mark beg of rnd.
Rnd 1 Purl.
Rnd 2 Knit, inc 1 st on each side of every corner st (M1, k1, M1).
Bind off all sts working (k1, p1) around.

Finishing
Weave in ends. Block lightly to measurements. ❖

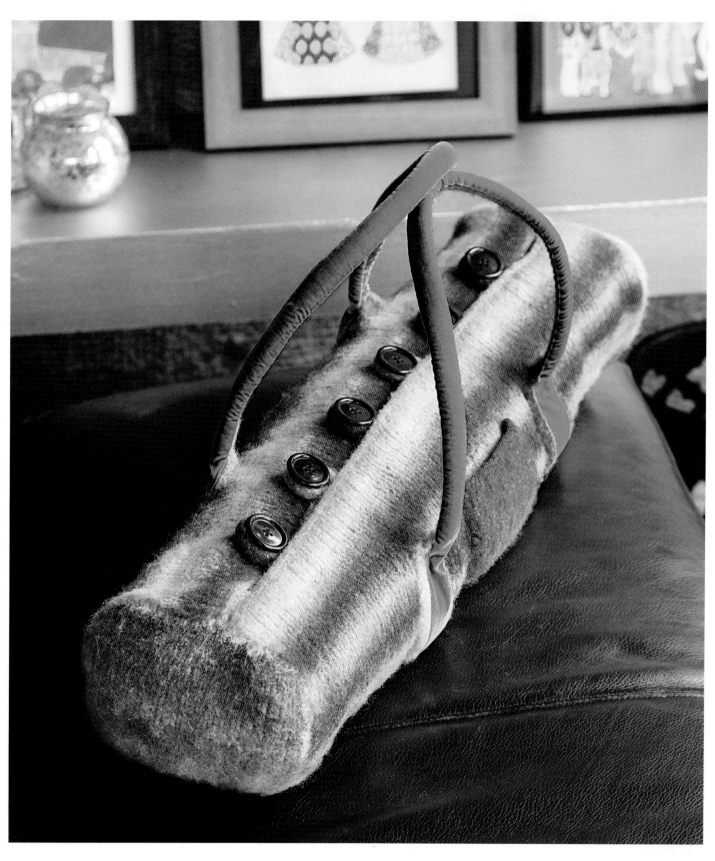

Stripes to Go

Stripes to Go

Designed by Jane Howorth

Colorful stripes, oversized buttons, bold shoulder straps, and a handy side pocket work together to make an unforgettable felted yoga mat bag.

Skill Level
■■□□

Knitted Measurements
Before felting approx 38"/96.5cm wide and 44"/112cm long
After felting approx 27"/68.5cm wide by 18"/46cm long
After assembly approx 27"/68.5cm wide by 7"/18cm wide by 5"/13cm tall

Materials
- 6 3½/100g hanks (each approx 109yd/99m) of Noro *Kureyon Air* (wool) in #319 Lime/Orange/Violet/Jade **⑥**
- One pair size 13 (9mm) needles, *OR SIZE TO OBTAIN GAUGE*
- Two size 13 (9mm) double-pointed needles (dpn)
- One size I/9 (5.5mm) crochet hook
- Removable stitch markers
- Scrap yarn
- 2½yd/2.25m decorative ribbon, 1½"/1.25cm wide
- Six 1½"/37.5mm buttons
- Sewing needle and thread

Gauge
8 sts and 11 rows to 4"/10cm over St st using size 13 (9mm) needles, before felting.
TAKE TIME TO CHECK GAUGE.

Note
Bag is felted after assembly. Buttons, ribbon, and felted button loops are attached after felting.

Bag
Cast on 76 sts.
Work 16 rows in St st (k on RS, p on WS), place B markers at beg and end of last row.
Work 28 rows in St st, place C markers at beg and end of last row.
Work 16 rows in St st, place D markers at beg and end of last row.
Work 16 rows in St st, place E markers at beg and end of last row.
Work 28 rows in St st, place F markers at beg and end of last row.
Work 16 rows in St st. Piece measures approx 44"/112cm from beg. Bind off.

End Panel (make 2)
Cast on 20 sts.
Work 28 rows in St st. Bind off knitwise on RS. Place A marker on bound-off edge between sts 10 and 11, place D marker on cast-on edge in same position. See Diagram 2 for placement of markers B, C, E, and F.

Handle
Using provisional cast-on (see page 142), cast on 6 sts.
Row 1 (WS) K1, p4, k1.
Row 2 Knit.
Rep rows 1 and 2 until piece measures approx 94"/239cm.
Place a marker at 47"/119.5cm. Carefully remove scrap yarn from cast-on edge and place sts on a dpn. Join last row to these sts using the 3-needle bind-off (see page 142).

Pocket
Cast on 16 sts. Work 22 rows in St st (k on RS, p on WS). Bind off.

Button Loop (make 6)
With dpn, cast on 4 sts and work I-cord for 18 rows (see page 142), piece measures approx 5½"/14cm. Bind off.

Finishing
Weave in ends. Place bag piece on table, RS up. Using diagram 1 as

DIAGRAM 1

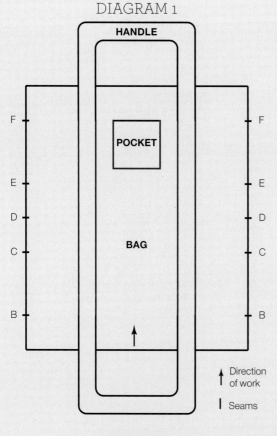

HANDLE

POCKET

BAG

F | F

E | E

D | D

C | C

B | B

↑ Direction of work

| Seams

DIAGRAM 2

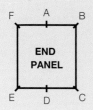

F   A   B

END PANEL

E   D   C

guide, place handle on top of bag with RS facing, and with handle seam and marker in line with D markers. With yarn and yarn needle, sew handle to bag between B and F markers, leaving handle free outside of those markers. With WS of handle facing, use yarn and yarn needle to seam the free side edges of the handle tog to create a tube.

Using diagram 1 as guide, place pocket between handles with RS facing. Sew in place with yarn, leaving top edge open. Sew top edge of pocket closed with sewing thread.

Sew one end panel to one side edge of bag, matching markers with cast-on and bound-off ends meeting at marker A. Sew rem end panel to other side edge of bag. Sew cast-on and bound-off edges of bag together for 2"/5cm from end panels, leaving center 32"/81.5cm free.

Machine felt (see page 142) assembled bag to 27"/68.5cm wide by 18"/46cm long, and felt the 6 button loops to 5"/13cm long. When dry, fold button loops in half and sew evenly spaced along WS of bound-off edge of bag opening. Carefully remove thread from top of pocket. Sew buttons to RS of cast-on side of opening, opposite loops. Begin and end at handle seam on underside of bag, sew ribbon along flat portion of handle, and sew ribbon around free portion of handle. ✤

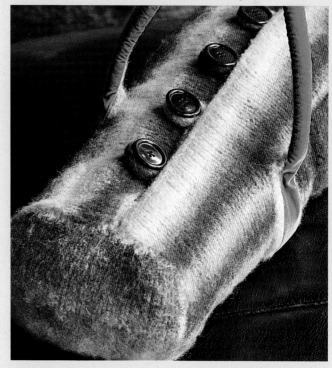

Rustic Ruana

Rustic Ruana

Designed by Cheryl Murray

A textural take on a traditional Latin American style utilizes moss stitch, diamond lattices, and broken ribbing.

Skill Level
■■■□

Size
Instructions are written for size Small/Medium.

Knitted Measurements
Width 33"/84cm
Length 28"/71cm

Materials
- 8 3½oz/100g hanks (each approx 109yd/99m) of Noro *Kureyon Air* (wool) in #263 Tomato/Black/Browns ⑥
- One pair size 15 (10mm) needles, *OR SIZE TO OBTAIN GAUGE*
- One size 15 (10mm) circular needle, 32"/80cm long
- Cable needle (cn)
- Stitch holder

Gauge
10 sts and 14 rows to 4"/10cm over St st using size 15 (10mm) needles.
TAKE TIME TO CHECK GAUGE.

Stitch Glossary
2-st RC Sl 1 st to cn and hold to *back*, k1, k1 from cn.
2-st RPC Sl 1 st to cn and hold to *back*, k1, p1 from cn.
2-st LPC Sl 1 st to cn and hold to *front*, p1, k1 from cn.

Moss Stitch
(odd number of sts)
Row 1 (RS) *K1, p1; rep from * to last st, k1.
Row 2 *P1, k1; rep from * to last st, p1.
Row 3 Rep row 2.
Row 4 Rep row 1.
Rep rows 1–4 for moss st.

Broken Rib
(odd number of sts)
Row 1 (RS) *K1, p1; rep from * to last st, k1.
Row 2 Purl.
Rep rows 1 and 2 for broken rib.

Back
Cast on 71 sts.
Work in moss st until piece measures 5½"/14cm from beg, end with a WS row.
Cont in St st (k on RS, p on WS) until piece measures 11"/28cm from beg, end with a WS row and inc 5 sts evenly across last row—76 sts.
Next row (RS) K1, work row 1 of chart 1 to last st, k1.
Next row P1, work row 2 of chart 1 to last st, p1.
Cont through row 17 of chart 1.
Dec row (WS) Purl, dec 5 sts evenly across row—71 sts.
Work in St st until piece measures 22"/56cm from beg, end with a WS row. Cont in broken rib until piece measures 28"/71cm from beg, end with a WS row.

DIVIDE THE FRONTS
Work 24 sts in broken rib and place sts on holder, bind off center 23 sts, then work rem 24 sts in established pat.

Left Front
Work 3 rows even.
Inc row (RS) K1, M1, work to end of row—1 st inc'd.
Note Work inc'd sts into pat.
Cont in broken rib, rep inc row every 4th row 6 times, then every other row 4 times—35 sts. AT SAME TIME, when left front measures 5½"/14cm, cont in St st for 6"/15cm, end with RS row.
Inc row 2 (WS) Purl, inc 3 sts evenly across—38 sts.

CHART 1

16 17
14 15
12 13
10 11
8   9
6   7
4   5
2   3
    1

6-st
rep

CHART 2

16 17
14 15
12 13
10 11
8   9
6   7
4   5
2   3
    1

6-st
rep

STITCH KEY

☐ k on RS, p on WS

⊟ p on RS, k on WS

⧓ 2-st RC

⧓ 2-st RPC

⧓ 2-st LPC

Next row K2, work row 1 of chart 2 to last 2 sts, k2.

Next row P2, work row 2 of chart 2 to last 2 sts, p2.

Cont through row 17 of chart 2.

Dec row (WS) Purl, dec 3 sts evenly across—35 sts.

Cont in St st until left front measures 22½"/57cm, end with a WS row.

Cont in moss st until left front measure 28"/17cm.

Bind off loosely in pat.

Right Front

Place sts for right front on needle ready to work a WS row.

Work 3 rows even.

Inc row (RS) Work to last st, M1, k1—1 st inc'd.

Note Work inc'd sts into pat.

Cont in broken rib, rep inc row every 4th row 6 times, then every other row 4 times—35 sts. AT SAME TIME, when right front measures 5½"/14cm, cont in St st for 6"/15cm, end with a RS row.

Beg with inc row 2 (WS), work same as left front.

Finishing

SIDE EDGINGS

With circular needle and RS facing, pick up and k 134 sts evenly along one side edge. Do *not* join.

Row 1 (WS) *P2, k2; rep from * to last 2 sts, p2.

Row 2 *K2, p2; rep from * to last 2 sts, k2.

Rep last 2 rows twice more. Bind off loosely in pat.

Rep for rem side edge.

FRONT AND NECK EDGING

With circular needle and RS facing, pick up and k 67 sts evenly along right front, 24 sts along back neck, and 67 sts evenly along left front—158 sts.

Beg with row 1 (WS), work same as for side edging.

Weave in ends. Block to measurements. ❧

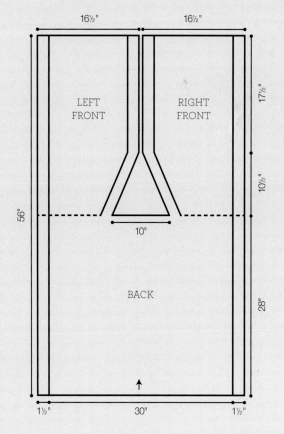

16½" 16½"

LEFT
FRONT

RIGHT
FRONT

17½"

10½"

10"

56"

BACK

28"

1½" 30" 1½"

↑ Direction of work

Top Notch

Top Notch

Designed by Jacob Seifert

Hat hair is a thing of the past when a ponytail or bun can sweep through luscious cables and out the other side.

Skill Level
■■■□

Knitted Measurements
Brim circumference 20"/51cm
Height 7¼"/18.5cm

Materials
■ 2 1¾oz/50g skeins (each approx 110yd/100m) of Noro *Kureyon* (wool) in #102 Pinks/Orange/Purple/Blue
■ One size 6 (4mm) circular needle, 16"/60cm long, *OR SIZE TO OBTAIN GAUGES*
■ One set (5) each sizes 5 and 6 (3.75 and 4mm) double-pointed needles (dpn)
■ One size G/6 (4mm) crochet hook
■ Scrap yarn
■ Cable needle (cn)
■ Stitch marker

Gauges
18 sts and 28 rows to 4"/10cm over St st using larger needles.
13 sts to 1½"/4cm over brim pat using larger needles.
TAKE TIME TO CHECK GAUGES.

Stitch Glossary
2-st RC Sl 1 st to cn and hold to *back*, k1, k1 from cn.
2-st LC Sl 1 st to cn and hold to *front*, k1, k1 from cn.
4-st RC Sl 2 sts to cn and hold to *back*, k2, k2 from cn.
4-st LC Sl 2 sts to cn and hold to *front*, k2, k2 from cn.
6-st RC Sl 3 sts to cn and hold to *back*, k3, k3 from cn.
6-st LC Sl 3 sts to cn and hold to *front*, k3, k3 from cn.

Brim Pattern
(13 sts)
Rows 1, 3, and 5 (WS) K1 (selvage st), p10, k2.
Row 2 (RS) K2, 4-st RC, k2, 4-st RC, p1 (selvage st).
Row 4 K6, 4-st RC, k2, p1.
Row 6 K4, 4-st RC, k4, p1.
Rep rows 1–6 for brim pat.

Body Pattern
(multiple of 26 sts)
Rnds 1 and 2 *P2, k1, p2, k4, p2, k9, p2, k4; rep from * around.
Rnd 3 *P2, k1, p2, 4-st RC, p2, 6-st RC, k3, p2, 4-st LC; rep from * around.
Rnds 4–6 *P2, k1, p2, k4, p2, k9, p2, k4; rep from * around.
Rnd 7 *P2, k1, p2, 4-st RC, p2, k3, 6-st LC, p2, 4-st LC; rep from * around.
Rnd 8 *P2, k1, p2, k4, p2, k9, p2, k4; rep from * around.
Rep rnds 1–8 for body pat.

Notes
1) Brim and body patterns can be worked from charts or written instructions.
2) Gauges are worked tighter than recommended for this yarn.

Hat
BRIM
With larger dpn, cast on 13 sts using the provisional cast-on (see page 142). Rep rows 1–6 of brim pat until piece measures 20"/51cm from beg, end with a RS row.
Remove scrap yarn from provisional cast-on, placing each released st on dpn. With RS held tog, use 3-needle bind-off (see page 142) to join cast-on sts with final row.

BEGIN BODY PATTERN
With RS facing and circular needle, beg at 3-needle bind-off, pick up and k 130 sts evenly around selvage st edge of brim, picking up sts inside of selvage st. Join to work in rnds and pm to mark beg of rnd. Work rnds 1–8 of body pat 3 times, then work rnds 1–3 once more.

CROWN SHAPING
Note Change to larger dpn when sts no longer fit comfortably on circular needle.

Dec rnd 1 *P2tog, k1, p2tog, k4, p2, k9, p2, k4; rep from *around —120 sts.

Rnd 2 *P1, k1, p1, k4, p2, k9, p2, k4; rep from * around.

Dec rnd 3 *P1, k1, p1, k4, p2tog, k9, p2tog, k4; rep from *around—110 sts.

Rnd 4 *P1, k1, p1, 4-st RC, p1, k3, 6-st LC, p1, 4-st LC; rep from * around.

Dec rnd 5 *P1, k1, p1, [k2tog] twice, p1, k9, p1, [k2tog] twice; rep from * around — 90 sts.

Rnd 6 *P1, k1, p1, k2, p1, k9, p1, k2; rep from * around.

Dec rnd 7 *P1, k1, p1, k2, p1, [k1, k2tog] 3 times, p1, k2; rep from * around—75 sts.

Rnd 8 *P1, k1, p1, 2-st RC, p1, 4-st RC, k2, p1, 2-st LC; rep from * around.

Dec rnd 9 *Sl 1 wyib, p2tog tbl, pass slipped st over p2tog, k2, p1, k6, p1, k2; rep from * around—65 sts.

Rnd 10 *P1, k2, p1, k6, p1, k2; rep from * around.

Dec rnd 11 *P1, k2, p1,[k2tog]3 times, p1, k2; rep from *around—50 sts.

RIBBED RIM

Change to smaller dpn.

Rnd 11 *K1, p1; rep from * around.

Dec rnd 12 *SK2P, [p1,k1] 3 times, p1; rep from * around—40 sts.

Bind off in rib.

Finishing

Weave in ends. ❖

BODY PATTERN

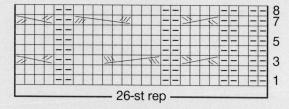

— 26-st rep —

BRIM PATTERN

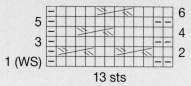

13 sts

STITCH KEY

☐ k on RS, p on WS   4-st RC

⊟ p on RS, k on WS   4-st LC

2-st RC   6-st RC

2-st LC   6-st LC

Country Weave Pillows

Country Weave Pillows

Designed by Rosann Fleischauer

A pair of big basketweave pillows make the perfect rustic yet airy home décor accent.

Skill Level
■■■□

Finished Measurements
22 x 22"/56 x 56cm after felting and assembly

Materials
■ 18 1¾oz/50g skeins (each approx 110yd/100m) of Noro *Kureyon* (wool) in #149 Brown/Grey/Taupe
■ One pair each sizes 9 and 11 (5.5 and 8mm) needles,
OR SIZE TO OBTAIN GAUGES
■ Cable needle (cn)
■ Yarn needle
■ Two 22"/56cm square pillows, covered in fabric to coordinate with yarn colors

Gauges
32 sts and 30 rows to 6"/15cm over basketweave pat st using larger needle, before felting.
16 sts and 20 rows to 4"/10cm over St st using smaller needle.
TAKE TIME TO CHECK GAUGES.

Basketweave Pattern Stitch
(multiple of 6 sts plus 2)
Rows 1 and 3 (WS) K1; wrapping each st twice, p to last st; k1.
Row 2 K1; *sl 3 sts and wraps to cn and hold to *back*; k3, dropping wraps; k3 from cn, dropping wraps; rep from * to last st, k1.
Row 4 K1; *sl 3 sts and wraps to cn and hold to *front*; k3, dropping wraps; k3 from cn, dropping wraps; rep from * to last st, k1.
Rep rows 1–4 for basketweave pat st.

Notes
1) Two identical pillows are made of 2 knitted pieces, a St st back and a felted basketweave st pat front. The pieces are joined, then a pillow already covered in coordinating fabric is inserted during finishing.
2) A garter st selvage is worked along the side edges of the back for seaming.

Back (make 2)
With smaller needles, cast on 86 sts.
Row 1 (WS) K1, p1, k to last 2 sts, p1, k1.
Row 2 Knit.
Row 3 Sl 1, k1, p to last 2 sts, k1, p1.
Row 4 Sl 1, k to end.
Rep rows 3 and 4 until piece measures 22"/56cm from beg, end with a RS row.
Work row 1 once more. Bind off.

Front (make 2)
With larger needles, cast on 116 sts. Work rows 1–4 of basketweave pat st 15 times, then work rows 1 and 2 once more. Bind off.

Finishing
Weave in ends. Block backs to measurements. Machine felt fronts (see page 142), block to measurements while still wet, and allow to dry completely. With WS of front and back held tog, sew top and side edges, working into garter st selvage sts on sides and rounding corners (see photos). Insert fabric-covered pillow. Sew final seam. Rep for 2nd pillow. ❖

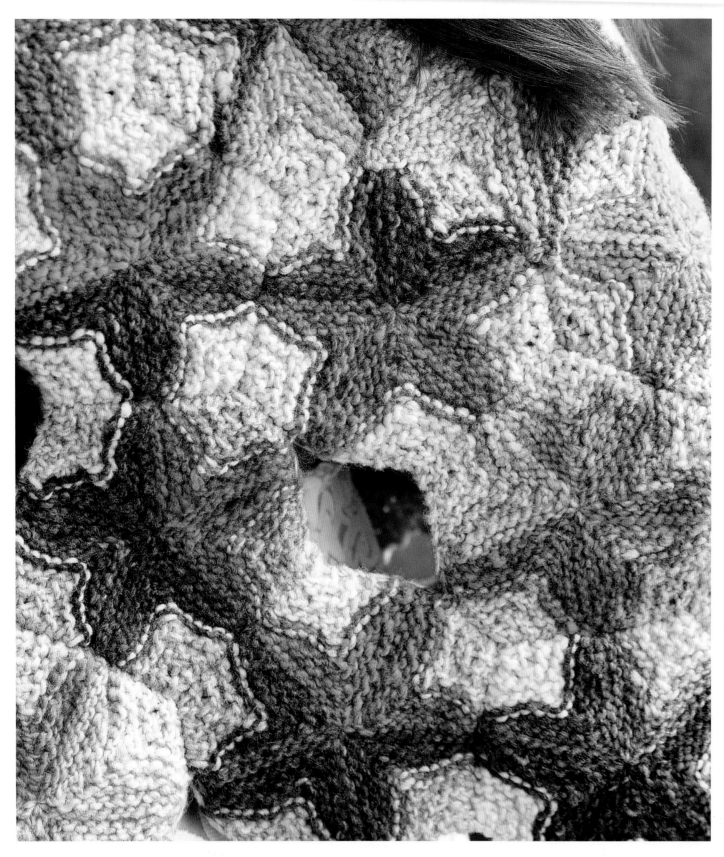

Starshawl

Starshawl

Designed by Unjung Yun

Sea-colored stars abut sandy diamonds in a shawl perfect for wrapping up in at the shore.

Skill Level
■ ■ ■ □

Knitted Measurements
Width at lower edge 52½"/133cm
Width at neck edge 25½"/65cm
Length 20½"/52cm

Materials
- 7 1¾oz/50g skeins (each approx 110yd/100m) of Noro *Kureyon* (wool) in #359 Blues/Lilac/Yellow (A) (④)
- 5 skeins in #211 Naturals (B)
- One set (4) size 9 (5.5mm) double-pointed needles (dpn), *OR SIZE TO OBTAIN GAUGE*
- One size 9 (5.5mm) circular needle, 24"/60cm long
- Stitch markers
- Two ⅔"/1.7cm sets of snaps

Gauge
16 sts and 32 rows to 4"/10cm over garter st using size 9 (5.5mm) needles.
TAKE TIME TO CHECK GAUGE.

Notes
1) For instructions on how to work short row wrap and turn (w&t), see page 142.
2) There are 39 small stars (S1–S39 on diagram), 3 big stars (Big Star on diagram), and 1 diamond (DB on diagram), all worked separately. After all pieces are worked, seam foll diagram and finishing instructions.

Small Star (make 39)
STAR CENTER
With circular needle and A, cast on 23 sts.
Row 1 (WS) Sl 1, k19, w&t.
Row 2 (RS) K7, SK2P, k7, w&t.
Row 3 K12, w&t.
Row 4 K3, SK2P, k3, w&t.
Row 5 K to end of row.
Row 6 Sl 1, k7, SK2P, k to end of row, pm—17 sts.
*Pick-up row (RS) With RS facing and using dpn, pick up and k 12 sts along left edge of piece just worked, then using knitted cast-on, turn and cast on 11 sts—23 sts.
Rep rows 1–5 with dpn.
Working sts onto circular needle, rep row 6 once more. Slide sts to middle of circular needle.
Rep from * twice more.
Next pick-up row (RS) With RS facing and using dpn, pick up and k 12 sts along left edge of piece just worked, then pick up and k 11 sts along right edge of first piece—23 sts.
Rep rows 1–5 once more.
Working sts onto circular needle, rep row 6 once more—85 sts on circular needle. Cut yarn.

DIAMOND FILLER
With B and RS facing, purl 1 rnd.
Fill in first 17-st section between star points, as foll:
Row 1 (RS) K1, k2tog, k4, SK2P, k4, ssk, k1—13 sts.
Rows 2, 4, and 6 Knit.
Row 3 K1, k2tog, k2, SK2P, k2, ssk, k1—9 sts.
Row 5 K1, k2tog, SK2P, ssk, k1—5 sts.
Row 7 K1, SK2P, k1—3 sts.
Row 8 SK2P. Fasten off last st.
Work each foll 17-st section between star points by rejoining B on the RS and working rows 1–8. After fastening off final st, use tail of A to close up holes in middle of star center, if needed.

Big Star (make 3)
With circular needle and A, cast on 27 sts.
Row 1 (WS) Sl 1, k23, w&t.
Row 2 (RS) K9, SK2P, k9, w&t.

Row 3 K16, w&t.

Row 4 K5, SK2P, k5, w&t.

Row 5 K8, w&t.

Row 6 K1, SK2P, k1, w&t.

Row 7 K to end of row.

Row 8 Sl 1, k8, SK2P, k to end of row, pm—19 sts.

***Pick-up row (RS)** With RS facing and using dpn, pick up and k 14 sts along left edge of piece just worked, then using knitted cast-on, turn and cast on 13 sts—27 sts.

Rep rows rows 1–7 with dpn.

Working sts onto circular needle, rep row 8 once more. Slide sts to middle of circular needle.

Rep from * twice more.

Next pick-up row (RS) With RS facing and using dpn, pick up and k 14 sts along left edge of piece just worked, then pick up and k 13 sts along right edge of first piece—27 sts.

Rep rows 1–7 once more.

Working sts onto circular needle, rep row 8 once more—95 sts on circular needle.

Bind off all sts.

Diamond

With B and dpn, cast on 17 sts.

Knit 1 WS row, then work same as rows 1–8 of diamond filler of small star.

Finishing

Foll diagram, seam pieces tog with seams on WS, then sew snaps in place.

Weave in ends. Steam lightly on WS. ❖

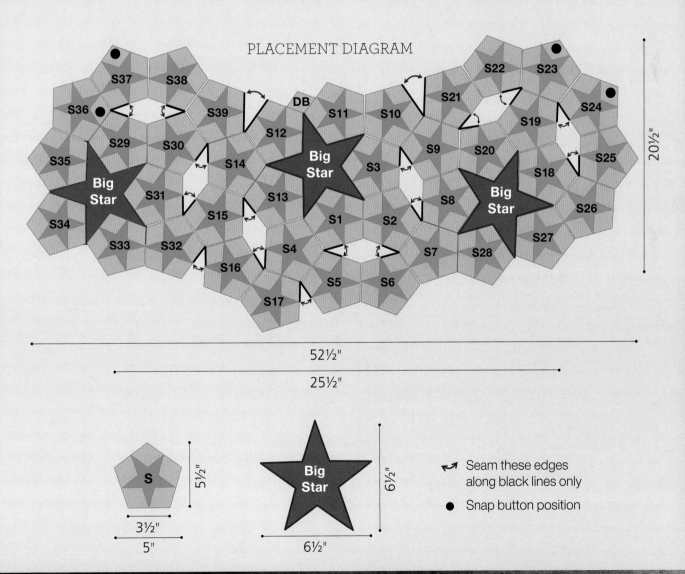

PLACEMENT DIAGRAM

↩ Seam these edges along black lines only

● Snap button position

Helpful Information

Abbreviations

approx	approximately
beg	begin(ning)
CC	contrasting color
ch	chain
cm	centimeter(s)
cn	cable needle
cont	continu(e)(ing)
dec	decreas(e)(ing)
dpn	double-pointed needle(s)
foll	follow(s)(ing)
g	grams
inc	increas(e)(ing)
k	knit
k2tog	knit 2 stitches together
kfb	knit into front and back
LH	left-hand
lp(s)	loop(s)
m	meter(s)
MB	make bobble
MC	main color
mm	millimeters
M1 or M1L	make one or make one left (see glossary)
M1 p-st	make 1 purl stitch (see glossary)
M1R	make one right (see glossary)
oz	ounce(s)
p	purl
p2tog	purl 2 stitches together
pat(s)	pattern(s)
pm	place marker

psso	pass slip stitch(es) over
rem	remain(s)(ing)
rep	repeat(s)(ing)(ed)
RH	right-hand
rnd(s)	round(s)
RS	right side
S2KP	slip 2 stitches together knitwise, knit 1, pass 2 slip stitches over knit 1 for a centered double increase
SK2P	slip 1 knitwise, knit 2 together, pass slip stitch over the knit 2 together for a left-slanting double increase.
SKP	slip 1 knitwise, knit 1, pass slip stitch over
sl	slip
sl st	slip stitch
sm	slip marker
ssk	slip, slip, knit (see glossary)
ssp	slip the next 2 sts one at a time purlwise to RH needle, insert tip of LH needle into fronts of these sts and purl them together
sssk	slip, slip, slip, knit (see glossary)
st(s)	stitch(es)
St st	stockinette stitch
tbl	through back loop(s)
tog	together
w&t	wrap and turn
WS	wrong side
wyib	with yarn in back
wyif	with yarn in front
yd	yard(s)
yo	yarn over needle
*	repeat directions following * as many times as indicated
[ ]	repeat directions inside brackets as many times as indicated

Checking Your Gauge

Make a test swatch at least 4"/10cm square. If the number of stitches and rows does not correspond to the gauge given, you must change the needle size. An easy rule to follow is:
To get fewer stitches to the inch/cm, use a larger needle; to get more stitches to the inch/cm, use a smaller needle. Continue to try different needle sizes until you get the same number of stitches in the gauge.

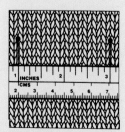

Stitches measured over 2"/5cm

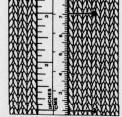

Rows measured over 2"/5cm

Skill Levels

■□□□
Beginner
Ideal first project.

■■□□
Easy
Basic stitches, minimal shaping, and simple finishing.

■■■□
Intermediate
For knitters with some experience. More intricate stitches, shaping, and finishing.

■■■■
Experienced
For knitters able to work patterns with complicated shaping and finishing.

Knitting Needle Sizes

U.S.	Metric	U.S.	Metric
0	2mm	9	5.5mm
1	2.25mm	10	6mm
2	2.75mm	10½	6.5mm
3	3.25mm	11	8mm
4	3.5mm	13	9mm
5	3.75mm	15	10mm
6	4mm	17	12.75mm
7	4.5mm	19	15mm
8	5mm	35	19mm

Glossary

as foll Work the instructions that follow.

bind off Used to finish an edge or segment. Lift the first stitch over the second, the second over the third, etc. (U.K.: cast off)

bind off in ribbing Work in ribbing as you bind off. (Knit the knit stitches, purl the purl stitches.) (U.K.: cast off in ribbing)

3-needle bind-off With the right side of the two pieces facing and the needles parallel, insert a third needle into the first stitch on each needle and knit them together. Knit the next two stitches the same way. Slip the first stitch on the third needle over the second stitch and off the needle. Repeat for 3-needle bind-off. (U.K.: 3-needle cast off)

cast on Place a foundation row of stitches upon the needle in order to begin knitting.

decrease Reduce the stitches in a row (that is, knit 2 together).

hold to front (back) of work Usually refers to stitches placed on a cable needle that are held to the front (or back) of the work as it faces you.

increase Add stitches in a row (that is, knit in front and back of stitch).

knitwise Insert the needle into the stitch as if you were going to knit it.

make one or make one left Insert left-hand needle from front to back under the strand between last stitch worked and next stitch on left-hand needle. Knit into back loop. One knit stitch has been added.

make one p-st With the needle tip, lift the strand between the last stitch worked and the next stitch on the left-hand needle and purl it. One purl stitch has been added.

make one right Insert left-hand needle from back to front under the strand between last stitch worked and next stitch on left-hand needle. Knit into front loop. One knit stitch has been added.

no stitch On some charts, "no stitch" is indicated with shaded spaces where stitches have been decreased or not yet made. In such cases, work the stitches of the chart, skipping over the "no stitch" spaces.

place markers Place or attach a loop of contrast yarn or purchased stitch marker as indicated.

pick up and knit (purl) Knit (or purl) into the loops along an edge.

purlwise Insert the needle into the stitch as if you were going to purl it.

selvage stitch Edge stitch that helps make seaming easier.

Standard Yarn Weight System

Categories of yarn, gauge ranges, and recommended needle and hook sizes

Yarn Weight Symbol & Category	0 Lace	1 Super Fine	2 Fine	3 Light	4 Medium	5 Bulky	6 Super Bulky	7 Jumbo
Type of Yarns in Category	Fingering 10-count crochet thread	Sock, Fingering, Baby	Sport, Baby	DK, Light Worsted	Worsted, Afghan, Aran	Chunky, Craft, Rug	Super Bulky, Roving	Jumbo, Roving
Knit Gauge Range* in Stockinette Stitch to 4 inches	33–40** sts	27–32 sts	23–26 sts	21–24 sts	16–20 sts	12–15 sts	7–11 sts	6 sts and fewer
Recommended Needle in Metric Size Range	1.5–2.25 mm	2.25—3.25 mm	3.25—3.75 mm	3.75—4.5 mm	4.5—5.5 mm	5.5—8 mm	8—12.75 mm	12.75 mm and larger
Recommended Needle U.S. Size Range	000–1	1 to 3	3 to 5	5 to 7	7 to 9	9 to 11	11 to 17	17 and larger
Crochet Gauge* Ranges in Single Crochet to 4 inch	32–42 double crochets**	21–32 sts	16–20 sts	12–17 sts	11–14 sts	8–11 sts	6–9 sts	5 sts and fewer
Recommended Hook in Metric Size Range	Steel*** 1.6–1.4 mm	2.25—3.5 mm	3.5—4.5 mm	4.5—5.5 mm	5.5—6.5 mm	6.5—9 mm	9—16 mm	16 mm and larger
Recommended Hook U.S. Size Range	Steel*** 6, 7, 8 Regular hook B-1	B-1 to E-4	E-4 to 7	7 to I-9	I-9 to K-10 1/2	K-10 1/2 to M-13	M-13 to Q	Q and larger

* GUIDELINES ONLY: The above reflect the most commonly used gauges and needle or hook sizes for specific yarn categories.

** Lace weight yarns are usually knitted or crocheted on larger needles and hooks to create lacy, openwork patterns. Accordingly, a gauge range is difficult to determine. Always follow the gauge stated in your pattern.

*** Steel crochet hooks are sized differently from regular hooks—the higher the number, the smaller the hook, which is the reverse of regular hook sizing

This Standards & Guidelines booklet and downloadable symbol artwork are available at: **YarnStandards.com**

slip, slip, knit Slip next two stitches knitwise, one at a time, to right-hand needle. Insert tip of left-hand needle into fronts of these stitches, from left to right. Knit them together. One stitch has been decreased.

slip, slip, slip, knit Slip next three stitches knitwise, one at a time, to right-hand needle. Insert tip of left-hand needle into fronts of these stitches, from left to right. Knit them together. Two stitches have been decreased.

slip stitch An unworked stitch made by passing a stitch from the left-hand to the right-hand needle as if to purl.

stockinette stitch Knit every right-side row and purl every wrong-side row.

work even Continue in pattern without increasing or decreasing. (U.K.: work straight)

work to end Work the established pattern to the end of the row.

yarn over Make a new stitch by wrapping the yarn over the right-hand needle. (U.K.: yfwd, yon, yrn)

Techniques

3-Needle Bind-Off

1) Hold right sides of pieces together on two needles. Insert third needle knitwise into first st of each needle, and wrap yarn knitwise.

2) Knit these two sts together, and slip them off the needles. *Knit the next two sts together in the same manner.

3) Slip first st on 3rd needle over 2nd st and off needle. Rep from * in step 2 across row until all sts are bound off.

Machine Felting

1) Use a low water setting and hottest temperature in a top-loading washing machine. Add small amount of laundry detergent and jeans or towels for agitation.

2) Place item in a lingerie bag or zippered pillowcase and add to machine. Check the felting progress frequently, removing item when the individual stitches are no longer visible and item is felted to the desired size.

3) Place item in cool water to stop the felting process and remove suds. Remove from bag and roll gently in towel to remove excess water.

4) Block and shape while wet. Pin into shape or stuff with plastic bags, and allow to air dry completely.

I-Cord

With 2 dpn, cast on required number of stitches, usually three to five. *Knit one row. Without turning the work, slide the stitches back to the opposite end of the needle to work next row from RS. Pull yarn tightly from the end of the row. Repeat from * to desired length.

Provisional Cast-On

Using scrap yarn and crochet hook, ch the number of sts to cast on plus a few extra. Cut a tail and pull the tail through the last chain. With knitting needle and yarn, pick up and knit the stated number of sts through the "purl bumps" on the back of the chain. To remove scrap yarn chain, when instructed, pull out the tail from the last crochet stitch. Gently and slowly pull on the tail to unravel the crochet stitches, carefully placing each released knit st on a needle.

Short Row Wrap & Turn (w&t)

On RS row (on WS row)
1) Wyib (wyif), sl next st purlwise.

2) Move yarn between the needles to the front (back).

3) Sl the same st back to LH needle. Turn work. One st is wrapped.

4) When working the wrapped st, insert RH needle under the wrap and work it tog with the corresponding st on needle.

Index

Distributors

To locate retailers of Noro yarns, please contact one of the following distributors:

USA
Knitting Fever Inc.
315 Bayview Avenue
Amityville, New York 11701
Tel: 001 516 546 3600
Fax: 001 516 546 6871
www.knittingfever.com

UK & EUROPE
Designer Yarns Ltd.
Units 8-10
Newbridge Industrial Estate
Pitt Street
Keighley BD21 4PQ
UNITED KINGDOM
Tel: +44 (0)1535 664222
Fax: +44 (0)1535 664333
Email: alex@designeryarns.uk.com
www.designeryarns.uk.com

GERMANY/AUSTRIA/
SWITZERLAND/BELGIUM/
NETHERLANDS/LUXEMBOURG
Designer Yarns (Deutschland) GMBH
Welserstrasse 10g
D-51149 Koln
GERMANY
Tel: +49 (0) 2203 1021910
Fax: +49 (0) 2203 1023551
Email: info@designeryarns.de

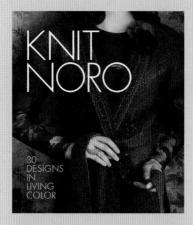
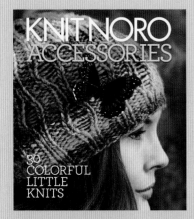
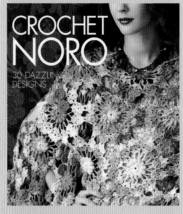

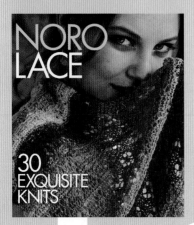

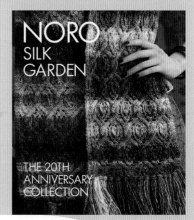

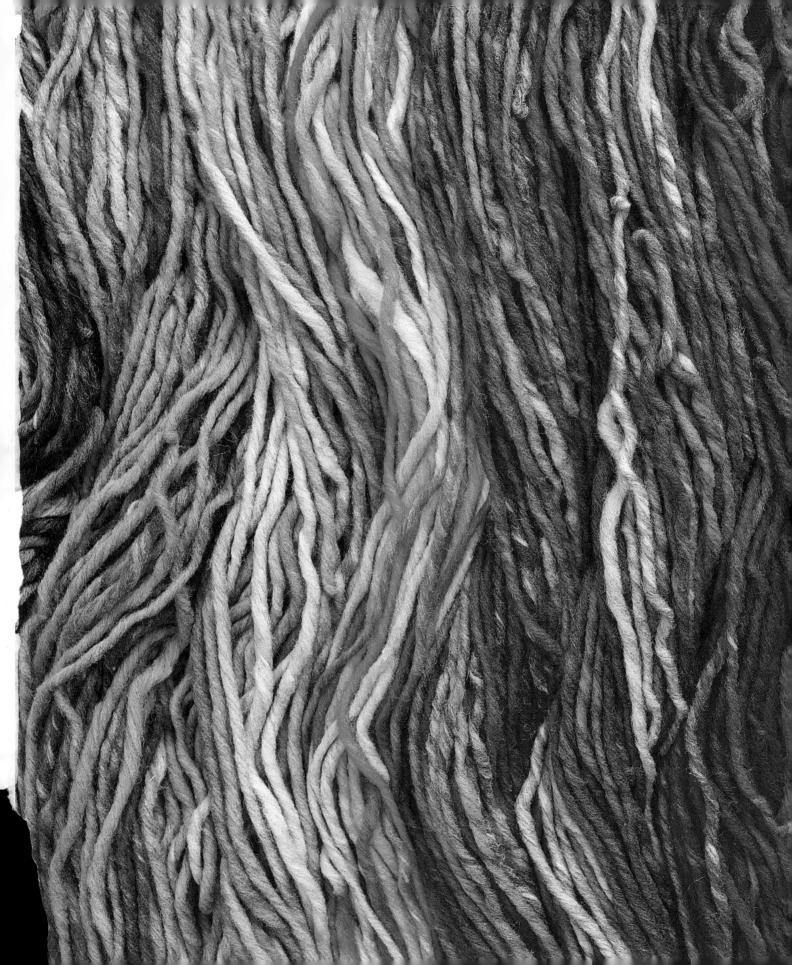